DIEGO HIDALGO

EUROPE:

Globalization and Monetary Union

Siddharth Mehta Ediciones
Madrid, 1998

© EMI: billete del euro
© Diego Hidalgo
Diseño Cubierta: Ángel Uriarte
ISBN: 84-86830-28-1
Depósito Legal: M-32357-98
Imprime: Artes Gráficas Hono, S.L.
Producción Editorial: avalon

CONTENTS

APOLOGIES AND THANKS

Widespread dismay was visible among my friends when they learned in February 1998 of my intention to publish this book. "Diego", some of them objected, "why are you publishing it now? Haven't you announced *The Future of Europe* for the summer of 1999?" Others, more resigned, offered these friendly warnings: "Well, go ahead and publish the book if you must. But don't write anything about Clinton and Monica Lewinsky or about the European Monetary Union, or we won't read it". Without too great a sacrifice, I managed to avoid writing about Monica Lewinsky. Unfortunately I could not avoid writing about the Monetary Union. I know I run the risk of losing many readers and perhaps even some friends. I ask their indulgence.

Although I cannot mention every person who helped me write this book, I must not forget to thank first of all Jesús Pérez, who was so helpful with *El Futuro de España* and with whom I am writing *The Future of Europe*. Juan Cruz, my publisher, was largely responsible for the success of *El Futuro de España*. Silvia Tedesco has been described as "a perfect angel" by several of the illustrious authors with whom I share the honor of being published by Siddharth Mehta. Angel Uriarte, artist, friend and collaborator during many years at Alianza Editorial, created the book's cover.

George Scialabba edited this book's English version, and Michael Hoch corrected it. Beatriz Iraburu, one of Europe's best journalists, read the manuscript and encouraged me not to throw it into the wastebasket. Bernie Barnett has also read my drafts. Bill Diamond, my former boss at the World Bank and the person from whom I have learned most in my professional life, has been a role model.

Charles Maier, Director of the Center for European Studies at Harvard University, has welcomed me as an associate since 1996. Jorge Domínguez, director, Anne Emerson, executive director, and Steve Bloomfield, Director of the Fellows Program at the Weatherhead Center of International Affairs, along with staff members Tricia Hughes and Jason Lambert, all gave me invaluable support during my stay at Harvard. Thanks also to the faculty of the Department of Political Science at the Graduate School and University Center of the City University of New York: W.W. Ofuatey-Kodjoe, my director of studies Christa Altenstetter, Hugo Kaufmann, who was kind enough to comment on my first draft, Kenneth Erickson, Juergen Dedring, David Meyer and William Tabb.

My colleagues from the Gorbachev Foundation will see their names mentioned in Chapter II of this book.

My wife Melania has helped me constantly, and has been my first reader and reviewer.

I. INTRODUCTION: REASONS FOR PUBLISHING THIS BOOK

Two years and a half have gone by since I wrote *El Futuro de España* –enough time to look back at a book about the future. The book's success was perhaps due more to brilliant promotion by the publisher, Juan Cruz of TAURUS, and to its opportune appearance just before the Spanish general elections of March, 1996, than to the merits of the book[1]. The book did, in any case, achieve most of the objectives I set forth in it. The main one was to present an accurate analysis of the current situation in Spain and the world viewed from the distance and perspective of Harvard University as well as from the familiarity provided by my close contact with Spanish institutions and people. My second objective was to draw attention to what I consider Spain's main problems and to suggest some solutions.

---

[1] The reviews were generally positive, although Javier Tussell wrote in *La Vanguardia* that my solutions to some problems were "utopian", and Darío Valcárcel wrote in *ABC* that the book contained "brilliant work, but a most unfortunate title ´El Problema de España´." Perhaps he read the book but not the title. On the other hand, Tom Burns, Madrid correspondent of the *Financial Times,* wrote in his own book *Conversaciones sobre el Socialismo* (Conversations about Socialism) "I consider Hidalgo's book a compulsory reading for every citizen".

These problems have to do with our integration into Europe, the proximity of the Maghreb and its explosive potential, the highest unemployment rate in Europe, a pension system facing almost certain bankruptcy, the poor quality of our universities, and the life tenure of civil servants in public administration. Many Spaniards would take issue with this list, others would add terrorism, and "uncontrollable nationalists whose unlimited demands will result in the disintegration of Spain". Despite the terrible events of the past two years, from the murder of Francisco Tomás y Valiente to the recent assassinations in 1998, I believe we will be able to solve these problems. I share the cautious optimism of Víctor Pérez Díaz, who recently remarked that Spain's future generations will be able to think automatically in three "keys" -the key of Europe, the key of Spain, and the key of Cataluña (or País Vasco or Extremadura) depending on the occasion.

At the beginning of my year in the Fellows Program at the Weatherhead Center for International Affairs at Harvard University in 1994, one professor told me unhesitatingly that I was bound to make a fool of myself by writing a book about the future, because all my predictions would fail. This was a plausible enough remark, because the future always has something unforeseeable in store. Nevertheless, I seem to have escaped making an entire fool of myself. Even though *El Futuro de España* discussed the likely evolution of the entire world, and not only Spain, only two major unanticipated events have occurred: the Asian crisis[2] and Spain's

---

[2] Actually, my book did warn about the risks that its "Ponzi style" financial system posed for Japan and for Asia: "Banks have too many debts, they have a weak

fulfillment of the Maastricht criteria for membership in the European Monetary Union, a possibility which seemed very remote in 1995.

These two unexpected events do not, I believe, affect the validity of my analysis in *El futuro de España*. We are still in my "Scenario 1" -Darwinian capitalism-, in which neoliberal market forces are irresistible. The United States continues to excercise political and economic hegemony throughout the world. In Spain, as the book predicted, Aznar won the elections of March of 1996 and was able to form a stable government even though lacking an absolute majority; while the Socialist Party continues to be in crisis and is unlikely to win the next general elections. The likelihood of Spain's improving its macroeconomic parameters enough to meet the Maastricht criteria seemed remote, but one of the scenarios at the end of the book acknowledged this possibility. On the other hand, the Aznar Government has done little or nothing to mitigate other basic problems: unemployment continues to be over 20%, the Pact of Toledo[3] does not resolve the pension system issue, the universities have not significantly improved, and the civil service employment rules are unchanged.

"Well, then", the reader may be asking him- or herself, "if the book published in 1996 still holds true, why write a new

---

structure, and the precedent of Daiwa Bank will be followed by other cases that will compel the Government of Japan to bridge the gap", *(El Futuro de España*, fifth edition, May 1996, p. 142)

[3]The "Pacto de Toledo" was an agreement on retirement pensions signed in 1994 by the main political parties in Spain. It establishes a gradual (and, in my view, futile) procedure for reducing pensions in the future, along with a promise that pensions will not be used as an electoral issue by the political parties endorsing the agreement.

11

one? Why not simply a new, updated edition?" One reason is that in Spain, as in other European countries, there are hardly any books about the European future. For some time I have been engaged in writing a book that will analyze the situation and prospects of Europe in the medium and long term and in a global context. I still consider that an urgent task and hope to publish that book in the main European languages by mid-1999.

Several other considerations, however, have led me to publish part of that book here and now. First, my recent work with the Gorbachev Foundation and the economists who collaborate in it has put me in touch with new ideas about economic globalization, which I believe are worth reporting. Second, I thought it is not only advisable but essential to reflect on the Monetary Union before the "train" departed in May 1998, when the European Union Council decided which among the Union's fifteen members will be entitled to ride, at least initially. Third, since the spring of 1997, I have been more and more alarmed by the euphoria exhibited in the Spanish media regarding our own economic situation and the outlook for Europe. In my opinion, this attitude is unwarranted and even potentially dangerous. Spain's fulfillment of the Maastricht criteria for admission to the Monetary Union is reason for satisfaction; the alternative would have been catastrophic. But this temporary victory over inflation and public deficits hardly assures smooth sailing for Spain.

There are three causes for concern that have been ignored by nearly all politicians, business leaders, the media, and consequently, by the electorate. The first is that few people have thought about how life will be in the Monetary Union. It is still not clear how "asymmetric shocks" -crises affecting some member countries of EMU and not others- are going to be resolved. The governments of the "shocked" countries will find themselves severely hampered in dealing with the crisis, having delegated their monetary policy to the European Central Bank, lacking labor mobility and fiscal flexibility, and with few possibilities for redistribution from the very small European Union budget. Some recent books, such as *The Single Currency: For and Against*[4], criticize the Monetary Union project and analyze its dangers; but even these do not frame the Euro within the context of the political economy of Europe during the next several years. On the other hand, some authors who have criticized the EMU have presented implausibly catastrophic scenarios. The most surprising example is Martin Feldstein, who predicts an intra-European war, perhaps even a war between Europe and the United States.[5]

Another source of concern is the medium - and long-term impact of the economic crisis in Asia, which began in the summer of 1997. This crisis arose out of a run on the currencies of some countries but worsened because of the absence of a national or regional lender of last resort. The International Monetary Fund came in for a lot of criticism

---

[4] Argentaria, Estudios de Política Exterior S.A. and Biblioteca Nueva, Madrid, 1997.

[5] Monetary Union in Europe and International Conflict, *Foreign Affairs,* Autumn 1997. Feldstein confirmed and extended in this analysis in a discussion with the Fellows of the Weatherhead Center for International Affairs of Harvard University, (February 27, 1998). Feldstein is Professor of Economics at Harvard University and President of the National Bureau of Economic Research. He was chairman of the Council of Economic Advisers in the Reagan Administration.

during this episode because it offered advice and tough conditions in place of a quick bailout or an injection of liquidity.

It would be unwise to suppose that Europe is immune to a similar crisis: only think of Banesto and Credit Lyonnais, among other examples. It is by no means certain that if a bank crisis took place in Europe, the European Central Bank would intervene to rescue the banks, shareholders, and investors of the affected country. How could it, without being accused of partiality and favoritism by the rest of the countries and by the competitors of those banks? I have seen very little thought about this potentially grave problem, though there is a fairly high probability of its arising.

But the main cause for concern is that the EMU is irrelevant to the most serious problems now looming in Europe. Not only will it resolve none of them, but it could even worsen many of them. Can anyone really believe that the single currency is going to solve not only unemployment and the insolvency of our pension systems, but even one of the problems listed below (Chapter IV)? European voters have not been given an opportunity to discuss the Euro, and in many countries they have been deceived; they have been forced to make sacrifices in order to "get to the finish line", which is what our admission into the Monetary Union is supposed to represent. If these citizens arrive at the finish line exhausted by the real or imagined effort they have made, and think that the economy will be a road of roses thereafter, how are they going to understand that their real effort begins now?

1. The Need for a Europe-Wide Analysis

In the Spanish literature on the current economic situation, Spain is always analyzed as if it were separate from Europe, and the latter as if it were isolated from the rest of the world. This lack of global vision is not uncommon, of course, but in my experience it is especially flagrant in Spain. Although the recent interest in the European Monetary Union has resulted in comparisons with other countries, these are usually limited to certain macroeconomic parameters: those concerned with the admission criteria determined by the Treaty of Maastricht, such as inflation and "fiscal health". It is rare to find an analysis of Spain in the European economy context or of Europe's competitiveness in the global economy.

This has several negative consequences. First and most obviously, it must result in irrelevant or even counterproductive conclusions and recommendations. Second, to take Spain as the unit of analysis reinforces our entrepreneurial isolation, a problem that Spanish companies have suffered for many years. It is an unfortunate fact -I could offer examples from many sectors- that Spanish companies "travel" worse than companies of other countries. Third, to speak of Europe without placing it in its world frame reinforces a similar problem: Europe's increasing endogamy and loss of touch with what is happening in the rest of the world.

For Europe, self-contemplation without global vision is a familiar and fateful mistake. In the 1990s, after the Cold War, Europe is in a crisis that can only be observed from the outside. This crisis is not only economic: as John Newhouse writes in the *Europe Adrift*[6]: «The threat of Moscow has been replaced by more traditional uncertainties - ethnic tensions, territorial controversies, short-sightedness, and lack of leadership. The context is similar to the one that preceded World War I: an unstable and chaotic Russia, a dominant Germany, tension and instability in the Balkans, an the inability of France and Great Britain, the oldest European nation-states, to act jointly in their own interest. In other words, Europeans appear to have a lack of purchase on events, and in that sense they are about where they were at the start of this century. One of the most apprehensive European characters, apprehensive about the future, Václav Havel, observes that 'Europe today lacks an ethos; it lacks imagination, it lacks generosity... Europe does not seem to have achieved a genuine and profound sense of responsibility for itself'». [7]

2. The Gorbachev Foundation

One day last year, I received a fax signed by Mikhail Gorbachev inviting me to collaborate in the work of his foundation, a "think tank" in which the problems of the future are analyzed and discussed: the dangers of nuclear, chemical and biological weapons, the deterioration of the environment, inter-cultural dialogue –especially between Islam and the West; the tragic crisis of Africa, the role of

---

[6]Europe Adrift, Pantheon Books, 1997, p 7

[7]Václav Havel, *How Europe can fail*, Lecture before the Council of Europe, Viena, November 9, 1993, quoted in New York Review of Books, November 18, 1993, p. 7.

Russia in the twenty-first century, and the benefits and dangers of economic globalization. Gorbachev referred to the future world scenarios presented in my book and asked me to join a permanent round table on globalization and its impact on national economies, which would meet for the first time at the end of 1997. The prospect of getting to know Gorbachev -an idol for my daughters Marta and Silvia, and a significant personality in the history of this century[8]- was irresistible and I accepted his invitation enthusiastically.

The group's exchange of ideas through e-mail, and above all the meetings held on the 15th and 16th of December, exceeded my expectations[9]. The Gorbachev Foundation's White Book on the dangers of uncontrolled globalization is still in preparation. However, I think that the six dangers identified there complement my analysis of Darwinian capitalism in *El futuro de España* and are worth noting here (a more extensive discussion follows in Chapter II):

---

[8] For me and for many people I know, Nelson Mandela and Mikhail Gorbachev are the last statesmen-heroes, the politicians who have succeeded most in changing the course of history in recent decades.

[9] The group that participated in the discussion presided over by Gorbachev included two Nobel laureates in economics (Lawrence Klein and James Tobin), two Indian economists (Jagdish Bhagwati and Muchkund Dubey), the Director of the Economic Institute of the Russian Academy of Sciences (Oleg Bogomolov), and other economists and political thinkers, such as Stanislas Menshikov and Alexandr Nekipelov (Russia), Mihaly Simai (Hungary), Victor Kovaldin, a political colleague of Gorbachev, Paul Welfens, a young German economist, Michael Intriligator of UCLA, Marshall Goldman, Director of the Russian Research Center at Harvard University, Reginald Dale, economics editor of the *International Herald Tribune,* and Diego Pizano, a Colombian economist.

a) unfair and unequal distribution of benefits and opportunities of globalization, and a corresponding increase of international and domestic inequality;

b) the survival of old monopolies and the formation of new ones, while the privatization of monopolies has increased their "perversity";

c) eroding of the sovereignty of nation-states (an assertion questioned by many, however, and even if true, not necessarily a danger, since it could have favorable effects);

d) the rapid spread of economic crises from one country to another, as shown by the domino-like collapse of several Asian economies in the last few months;

e) the uncontrolled mobility and concentrations of short-term and speculative capital which contributes to the building of "houses of cards" that, while appearing solid, may crumble easily; this increases volatility and uncertainty, and therefore the instability of the world economy;

f) the chance that globalization will destroy "growth engines": economies that pulled the others forward, as is the case of Germany in Europe, and with Japan in Asia.

3. Economic Triumphalism

Ever since its formation in May 1996, the major priority of the Aznar Government has been to fulfill the Maastricht criteria in order to be admitted to the European Monetary Union. The anti-inflationary methods of the Banco de España have had a resounding and unprecedented success. At first, the fiscal measures included minor cuts in spending, some cosmetic changes and one-time privatizations. However, with the help of a higher-than-expected economic growth and thus greater tax receipts, a lower numerator (budget deficit) and greater denominator (GNP) in the deficit/GDP ratio, and, most importantly, the convergence of interest rates with the prevailing European rates, which have lowered the interest costs of the public debt by more than two trillion pesetas, cosmetic measures are no longer necessary. Spain passes the Maastricht test with a "B+". This is an important achievement, which eighteen months ago would have been considered utopian.

On the other hand, the government has done nothing about urgently-needed structural measures (pension reform, improvements in university and public administration). Moreover, unemployment in Spain is still close to 20%, and the agreement between CEOE (the Spanish confederation of entrepreneurs) and the labor unions is insufficient to generate significant employment creation. This is not a criticism of the Spanish government; it is conceivable that a suitable political opportunity to undertake these unpopular reforms has not yet appeared. As for unemployment, although Spain's is the highest in Europe, it has nonetheless decreased in some measure even though it has increased in France, Germany and Italy. Still, it is a fact that 90% of the structural reforms needed in the Spanish economy have not begun.

The Spanish government made a wise decision (as did most of countries in Europe) by giving priority to qualifying for the Monetary Union, and it has reaped the benefits with a virtuous circle: less inflation, lower interest rates, lower debt-service payments, and a sharply reduced budget deficit. The government sought admission to the Monetary Union mainly for fear of being left out; and indeed, life outside the Monetary Union would be intolerable. But life inside the EMU will also be very difficult, as we shall see.

Nevertheless, since the fall of 1996, a few months after the Aznar government was formed, the media have been bombarding Spaniards with messages which are more and more triumphalist. It is true that the Monetary Union has already benefited Spain significantly by producing the virtuous circle just mentioned. It is also true that the economy has grown and that growth prospects in the immediate future appear excellent. However, our medium-term prospects are less certain.

The government's attitude, claiming all the credit for such good macroeconomic news and for membership in EMU, is understandable; what I find hard to understand is the silence of the opposition and the exaggerated optimism of the media, normally critical of the government.

This triumphalist propaganda has had two pernicious effects. One has been to cause everyone to forget the urgent need to undertake structural reforms (making the labor market more flexible in order to generate employment, changing the pension system in order to make it viable, drastically improving the university system in order to upgrade our human capital, giving young people better job opportunities, and reforming public administration). The other has been to misrepresent the Monetary Union as a magic solution to all our problems, thereby creating expectations which cannot be met.

Even if the EMU proves to be a success, it is unlikely to solve Europe's problems, as I will argue in Chapter IV. The consequences of the resulting disappointment are not unpredictable: there may well be serious nationalist and anti-European movements, as politicians find it irresistible to blame "Europe". Because the EMU has been presented as a panacea, particularly in southern Europe, anti-European centrifugal reactions are all too likely.

Surprisingly, triumphalism marks the response not only to the course of Spanish economy, but also to the economic success of the European Union and the prospects of the Euro[10]. This contrasts with the prevailing extremely pessimistic opinion of the EMU and Europe's prospects among American economists. Doomsaying is far from my intention, and I think that some tragic prophecies about the Monetary Union and the Euro by critics such as Jeffrey Sachs go too far. Nevertheless I believe that Europe's situation does not warrant enthusiastic bell-ringing either.

---

[10]In his articles about the World Economic Forum in Davos at the end of January, Xavier Vidal Folch assured the readers of *El País* that the Euro is a serious threat to the dollar as a reserve currency and that Americans generally consider Europe the part of the world with the best economic outlook. On the same day I read these articles (January 27, 1998), I attended a conference organized by Harvard University in which much of the academic and financial elite of the United States came to totally opposite conclusions. In Chapter IV, I will outline the arguments and conclusions of this conference.

As argued in subsequent chapters, Europe has a long list of structural problems that will not be resolved by the EMU. These problems include, for example, high production costs, which might be reduced by the European Central Bank with a policy of a weak Euro. But most of Europe's economic problems cannot be solved by the Monetary Union. Among these are a lack of business dynamism, high unemployment (whose social effects are currently mitigated by benefit levels that will be unsustainable in the future), technological backwardness in sectors crucial for the future, an aging population, bankrupt pension systems, and disagreements about national and foreign policy issues among Europe's member states.

4. The EMU Begins

On May 2 and 3, the Council of Ministers of the European Union met to decide, by qualified majority, which countries beginning on January 1, 1999, will be members of the Monetary Union. This decision, which a year ago appeared uncertain and dramatic, gradually lost its uncertainty. All the countries of the Monetary Union except Greece were judged to have fulfilled the Maastricht criteria.

The EMU has fervent defenders in Europe, as well as passionate critics. There is no doubt that it will be a milestone in the history of European integration, or that it will produce drastic changes in everyday economic and political life of all our countries. Its enthusiasts hope that monetary union will gradually bring greater political union among countries. Its opponents predict that it will lead to growing tension, and that its final effect will be serious divisions within the European Union. For a year and a half I have been reflecting on the EMU and listening to the opinions of distinguished economists, political scientists, and other students of Europe. I believe that this is the moment to synthesize these reflections.

Almost all economists agree that, economically, the Monetary Union is at best a zero-sum game, that is, its benefits for European countries will be more or less equal to its costs. Its contribution should therefore be estimated on the basis of its potential political effects. This book raises a series of issues that, in my opinion, underlie our European discussion but are seldom clearly articulated.

I intend to raise four sets of questions:

1. Europe has many problems on its horizon. What are the main ones, how serious are they, and what is their prognosis? Will the EMU help solve these problems?

2. What are the benefits and costs of the EMU? What opportunities and risks it present to the Europeans?

3. Is the trend toward transferring sovereignty to the European Central Bank, which is what the EMU implies, compatible with the even stronger trend towards decentralization and with the slowing EU's political integration reflected, for example, in the Treaty of Amsterdam?

4. Which measures should Europe take in order to make a good ecoonomic start in the twenty-first century?

II. AN OVERVIEW OF GLOBALIZATION

1. What is Globalization?

The term "globalization" has become specially fashionable since the end of the Cold War. The concept has supporters and opponents, and there is disagreement about what it really means [11]. Professor Intriligator affirms that "globalization is a powerful real aspect of the new world system, and one of the most influential forces in determining the future of the planet". Mihaly Simai defines it as a higher level of "internationalization": the flow of goods, service, capital, people, information and technology; the prevalence of an orientation toward free markets, investments and other business transactions; geographical and institutional integrational of markets, and the emergence of global problems that require a world cooperation. I would emphasize the growing interdependence of national economies produced by a new and unique economic system in which everyone competes not only within national boundaries but also - more and more - across them. This interdependence is represented in international trade, capital flows and technology.

---

[11] At the Gorbachev Foundation conference, each of the participants offered a different definition.

In the academic writing, the use of the concept "globalization" leads to controversy. Critics of the concept affirm that globalization has existed from time immemorial, and that little or nothing has changed in recent times. Perhaps the best known of these critics is Stephen Krasner of Stanford University.

Some Euro-centered views place the origins of globalization in the late fifteenth and early sixteenth century, when great geographic discoveries connected Europe with other continents. Other see its origin in a pre-Columbian global economy [12]. Still others propose an Asian rather than a European focus. Some writers influenced by Marxism deny the existence of globalization, insisting that only flows of speculative and short term capital have grown in geometric progression, while international trade in goods and services and productive foreign investment have increased only moderately in recent years. Some British intellectuals have suggested that globalization is little more than a return to the world economy of the late nineteenth century, a period in which there were important international movements of capital and population, the most important countries of Europe depended on international commerce, and the British Empire controlled the world economy.

Although some observers may have prematurely announced that the world has turned into a global village, it

---

[12] Andre Gunder Frank: *Global Economy in the Asian Age,* University of California Press, 1998, quoted in Stanislav Menshikov's paper *Indicators and Trends of Globalization* presented at the Conference on Economic Globalization organized by the Gorbachev Foundation in December 1997.

is hard to deny the existence of globalization or the fact that the changes under way at the end of the twentieth century are, in important ways, new. At any rate, it is one premise of my argument that no country or region can be analyzed except in a global context whose significance continues to increase.

Several factors accelerate the process of economic globalization:

1. The technological revolution, comparable in magnitude and effects to the industrial revolution of the nineteenth century, has reduced transport and communication costs dramatically. E-mail, the Internet and the World Wide Web have brought all the countries in the world nearer one another. At present, one can buy for less than $2,000 a laptop computer millions of times more powerful than the mainframe computers for which the World Bank, in the 1970s, paid seven thousand times as much.

2. The fall of the Berlin Wall in 1989, the end of the Cold War, and the dissolution of the Soviet Union in 1991 completed a process of cataclysmic change that began in China with Deng's economic reform in 1978. (An important milestone for this process, frequently missed by historians, was the disastrous failure of François Mitterrand's economic policy in France from his election in May, 1981 until the fall of Pierre Mauroy's government in 1983 and the departure of its four communist ministers). The result of this change was a world-

wide ideological convergence toward free markets and free-trade. The only two remaining Communist countries with centrally planned economies, Cuba and North Korea, are suffering a serious decline in their standard of living and will probably end up abandoning their philosophy and system. The other Communist countries –China, Vietnam, Russia, Eastern European countries and the old Soviet Socialist Republics– plus socialist India, with half the world's population (roughly two and a half billion) people between them, have joined the capitalist world and compete with Europe, America, and Japan, in the global market.

3. Multinational enterprises have grown remarkably during the past two decades, increasing their contribution to Gross World Product. Formerly, these companies had a "multi-market" strategy: their position in a country was not determined by their position in others. Nowadays, the number of multinational enterprises whose competitiveness and strategy in one country are conditioned by their position in other countries is far higher. These companies have increased their power, sales, profits and productivity thanks to their ability to choose their factors of production from many countries. A clue to the growing importance of this global strategy is the fact that internal trade within these companies represents almost a third of total world trade.

4. Other factors that contribute to globalization are the trend toward increased liberalization of international

trade, the institutionalization of GATT in the WTO, the homogenization of media, and the predominance of English as a global language.

Along with freer trade, globalization implies increasingly tough competition among all countries and blocs. A larger share of every country's markets will be submitted to this fierce competition. Protectionism and subsidies in this world order are futile and are condemned to disappear.

Globalization brings great benefits; the growth of national economies caused by foreign investment and exports; productivity increases; lower prices. It can also, however, bring unfairness, inequality and instability. Should we try to contain or roll back globalization? My answer is no, unless a global crisis occurs in which all countries simultaneously find themselves compelled to change the system -a remote contingency. No country is big enough to resist or small enough to evade globalization, or to rewrite the rules of the game. The collapse of the Soviet Union and the impoverishment of Cuba (due only in part to the economic blockade by United States and the halt in Soviet subsidies) and of North Korea, are clearly examples of the futility of any such attempt.

The diatribes of some writers against "neoliberalism" inherent to globalization do, it is true, have some ethical force. Darwinian capitalism is not indefinitely sustainable or desirable. In the very long term, perhaps after some far-off global crisis, it will yield place to a new world order, more regulated and fair. Until then, however, frontal resistance, or the attempt to find the " European third way" sought for in vain by the French socialists, is futile.

It is essential to begin from this premise when analyzing the prospects of Europe or assessing the effects of the Monetary Union, which is why I have spent so much time in this chapter restating the obvious. Europe cannot become a protectionist fortress; the walls of this fortress will end up crumbling; the sand castle will lie in ruins for decades; and our children and our grandchildren will either will be impoverished or forced to emigrate. The decision to compete, both in other markets and in our own, greatly limits our ideologic and political options.

2. Dangers of Globalization. The Gorbachev Foundation

I have already mentioned the first Conference of the Gorbachev Foundation, which took place under the chairmanship of Mikhail Gorbachev in December, 1997. Our objective was to identify the main problems caused by economic globalization, and to discuss the options available to governments and international organizations. Preparatory work for the conference started in the spring of 1997, before the economic crisis in Asia broke out; and although we tried to learn from that crisis, the participants examined trends at medium and long term instead of reacting to recent events. In this chapter, I will identify six troubling and possibly dangerous trends.

A. Inequalities

In my view the main problem of globalization is the unequal distribution of its costs and benefits. It produces winners and losers, both within countries and internationally. In advanced countries like the United States, global competition, technological advances, and the importance of new computing technology, have a number of inequality-enhancing effects. First, they increase the remuneration of the elite who specializes in rapid growth sectors, such as finance, investing and computing. Second, they enrich the owners and shareholders of those companies whose stock values have increased spectacularly during the last decade [13]. Third, they cause dramatic downsizing. Fourth, they generate many jobs in non-specialized services with very low wages.

Only countries able to compete internationally can prosper. Technology causes the terms of trade of the producers of raw material to deteriorate. These producers constantly see the price of traditional exports reduced, and their products sometimes replaced altogether by other products that result from new technologies. While the industrialized countries and some developing countries flourish in this environment, many countries in Africa, the Middle East and even Asia have lower per capita incomes at present than twenty-five years ago. Entire continents like Africa remain marginal to the world economy.

I should note that the hypothesis that globalization leads to inequalities, which I am attempting to establish in my doctoral dissertation at City University, was not shared by most for the participants of the Conference [14]. However, they did

---

[13] In 1997, the aggregate price of stocks of a single company (both Intel or Microsoft, actually) was already twice the total of the whole American automobile industry (General Motors + Ford + Chrysler). Not many years ago, General Motors was the biggest company in the world.

[14] Both Muchkund Dubey (India) and Diego Pizano (Columbia) were against admitting increased inequalities as a proven consequence of globalization. Dubey

not succeed in refuting it either, and Gorbachev included it in his own conclusions.

Although many Africans reject the idea that their continent has been marginalized by the system, it is obvious that the gap between industrialized countries and Africa has increased enormously during the last twenty-five years. When I began working at the World Bank in 1968, the average income of one European was equivalent to that of eleven Africans. In 1998, this figure has increased to 45; according to the Bank's current forecast, and considering that Africa's population will triple in the next forty years, in 2035 a European will earn more than 110 Africans.

In Africa there are more than 100 million people with incomes equivalent to less than $0.20 a day; the average income of an American is 600 times higher. According to one of the Conference participants, the President of Nike earns more than the sum of the wages of his 15,000 workers in Indonesia. I could quote many more shocking statistics to prove that globalization creates winners and losers, increases unfairness and inequalities, and leads to the exploitation of the poorest countries by the richest. Unlike many of my colleagues, I think that the differences in wealth and income between poor and rich are an urgent problem. The argument that "there have always been poor people" –frequently invo-

---

argued that India has improved its position in the world and has reduced its difference with industrialized countries "thanks to globalization", while Pizano affirmed that the worsening of global income distribution is still under study among economists. I was pleased, however, that Gorbachev included my reasoning when presenting his conclusions to the press and emphasized this point as the first danger of globalization. Darwinian capitalism is producing winners and losers; and as Engels said, the losers will end up ruining the winners´party.

ked to quiet individual consciences– is not valid; differences not only among individuals but also among countries are increasing. This unequal distribution of the benefits of globalization is one of the main problems and challenges for the world in the twenty-first century.

At the same time I am not at all sure that increasing aid to the Third World, at least the way the current system dispenses it, is the solution to the problems of the loser countries. I cannot pursue the subject here; but I hope the Gorbachev Foundation and similar forums will give it priority in their search for new solutions.

Another disputed question is whether globalization increases inequalities in the distribution of incomes within countries. The worsening of income distributions is one the most serious problems faced by the United States. In Europe –except for Great Britain– and Japan, distribution has apparently not deteriorated, probably because of the redistributive policies of those governments. In most of Latin America, the Middle East, and Africa, differences in income between the elite (the top 5% or so) and the rest of the population are widening. These countries are faced with serious unemployment among the young, and extremely serious deficiencies in primary and secondary education that threaten to perpetuate this problem. Although few would question the existence of these inequalities, whether they are a consequence of globalization is more controversial.

B. Perceived Loss of National Sovereignty

Some observers believe that as a result of globalization, states are gradually losing their sovereignty, handing it over

to other entities, whether more powerful states, multinational companies, or supranational organizations. This is the
case with European Union countries within the institutions
of Brussels and Strasbourg; the issue arises again when the
countries entering the EMU delegate their monetary sovereignty to the European Central Bank. The United States
Congress had difficulty, based on fears of a possible loss of
sovereignty, in ratifying NAFTA (North American Free
Trade Agreement) and approving U.S. adhesion to the
WTO.

Among the visionaries who predict the decline and
extinction of the nation-state that emerged from the Treaty of
Westfalia in 1648 are well-known authors such as John
Naisbitt, Norman Macrae and Robert Kaplan. The essence of
their argument is that governments are gradually being dis-
credited and losing their power; the greater the expectations
they raise among citizens, the greater their discredit, given
their inability to satisfy these expectations [15]. The belief that
states are losing sovereignty is based on other reasons as
well: [16]

a) Multinational companies have more and more power
and weight in the world economy; their transnationality
enables them to avoid border controls and state jurisdictions; the growth of their power is inversely proportional to that of states;

---

[15] Naisbitt predicts a world with a thousand countries in the twenty-first century;
Macrae, the total privatisation of states; and Kaplan, the spread of anarchy and
chaos.

[16] Cf. "Scenario "3", El Futuro de España, p. 54-58.

b) States are trapped between two contradictory trends: globalization, which means delegating power to supranational organizations, and nationalism and regionalism, which lead to decentralization and the increasing loyalty of individuals to smaller communities;

c) New means of communication (Internet, World Wide Web) are uncontrollable by states and enable individuals to operate outside the rules established by those states;

d) International financial markets are not controlled by either states or central banks and are able to bring down monetary parities, to ignore agreements fixed by central banks, and even to ruin apparently solid economies;

e) The trend towards privatization of public enterprises and government agencies leads to a decrease of government size, with a corresponding decline in state's power. [17]

f) The tax incomes of most states are in permanent decline and will gradually run out as private companies and individuals are able to choose the fiscal jurisdiction under which they will pay their taxes; this will force

[17] According to Norman Macrae, former editor of *The Economist,* who in 1975 predicted the fall of Berlin Wall in 1989, "human beings are intelligent and are starting to realize that governments always do everything worse than individuals or private sectors; governments will be forced to reduce their size and will end up disappearing". Conference in Mexico D.F. in 1993.

states to compete fiscally among themselves with a resulting drastic decrease in their income and spending capacity.

These trends appear plausible enough, and I do not dismiss the possibility of their having important consequences in the future. Nevertheless, I think that there is evidence that they are not yet significantly eroding the powers of the nation-state. While I am obviously a firm believer in the reality of globalization, I also think there are frequent illusions or exaggerations about the pace at which it is proceeding. The belief that there is a very rapid trend towards privatization has been recently refuted by several authors, and specially by *The Economist* of September 20-26, 1997, an issue dedicated specifically to this topic. Their statistics show that, despite all the processes mentioned above, the percentage of GNP going through states not only has not decreased, as one might expect, but has increased since the end of the Cold War. As I have heard more than one lecturer affirm, "reports of the nation-state's demise have been greatly exaggerated".

C. Vulnerability to the Contagion of Economic Crises

As has been demonstrated recently in Asia, a financial crisis in one country can quickly affect others. A crisis in a relatively small country, like Thailand, with a GNP of $120 billion, can threaten a much more significant economy like South Korea's, with a GNP of $500 billion, and can even affect a great power like Japan, with a GNP of $4 trillion. A "virus" in one country can spread to a whole continent and even result in a global crisis. The economic interdependence among countries makes their mutual vulnerability much greater.

The virus is transmitted by speculative capital flows, which travel toward countries with a current account deficit (i.e., short-term debts exceed realizable assets), which was the case in five of the countries most affected by the crisis: South Korea, Indonesia, Malaysia, Thailand and Philippines. The crisis has not affected in the same way countries such as China, Singapore, and Taiwan, which are able to finance their investments with internal savings, foreign investment, and long-term debt. These countries were "vaccinated" against the virus, converting their speculative capital flows into reserves instead of investing them.

D. Weakness Produced by the International Financial Markets

The mobility and concentrations of short term and speculative capital reinforce the tendency toward "houses of cards" which, while apparently solid, readily collapse; this increases changeability and uncertainty, and therefore, the instability of the global economy. The tremendous problems that have devastated the economies of Thailand, Malaysia, and Indonesia as a result of the frenetic movements of short-term capital towards these countries in 1995 and 1996, and its sudden flight since June, 1997, are an example of the vulnerability that speculative flows of capital can produce.

In small countries, capital markets are modest and fragile, which means that this type of crisis can be very difficult to counteract. When hordes of speculators want to sell at the same time, prices have to fall abruptly before buyers who can stabilize them show up. The memory of "Black Monday" of the New York stock market on October 1987 is recent enough to remind us that panics may take place even in the much larger capital markets of industrialized countries.

How can we encourage long-term investment and discourage speculative capital movements? One measure, on a national basis, would be to make capital-gains taxes be inversely proportional to the length of the investment. Another would be to impose a tax on every transaction, small enough not to be a hindrance to investment and to capital movements, but large enough to generate significant amounts, reduce the tremendous volatility of speculative capital, and allow greater international differences in the rate of interest. (This proposal is sometimes known as the "Tobin Tax", after James Tobin who has been proposing it since 1971).

The so called "Washington Consensus", i.e. the position of the international lending organizations (International Monetary Fund and World Bank) supported by the U.S. President and Congress, opposes the Tobin Tax or any regulation of capital flows. However, the Asian crisis is a very powerful argument for reconsidering the IMF's position. The question is no longer whether it is proper to regulate capital flows, but how to do so. [18]

E. Are Monopolies Growing?

The issue, presented in the Conference's press release with a question mark, is whether the growth and geographic

---

[18] This is the title of Martin Wolf's article in the *Financial Times,* March 3rd, 1998, page 16.

expansion of transnational companies are leading to the establishment of global monopolies. Microsoft, now (1998) being investigated by the Anti-trust authorities in the United States, is one example.

The persistence of old monopolies and the formation of new ones have not been successfully controlled. The privatization of monopolies has increased the perversity of their effects: privatized companies remain as monopolies and act as such when setting prices that give them huge margins, but because they are private and no longer accountable to electorates, they can remove unprofitable parts from their operations and therefore cut or eliminate services which are essential to citizens. For example, a railroad monopoly or an electricity company could cut services that are not profitable but are important for the survival of towns or entire regions, and whose elimination could harm not only the affected, but the country as a whole.

F. Can Economic Growth Rates Be Maintained?

The issue is whether the Gross World Product will increase or decrease in the future as a result of globalization. Former "engines of growth" such as Japan, the "Asian Tigers" and Germany have seen their economic growth rates peak and fall; they can no longer provide a pull for the rest of their regions and for the world economy. Could these economies regain their old growth rates? Will other "engines" emerge?

My colleagues from the Conference mencionated as candidates for future "engines" Latin America and Eastern

Europe. In our post-conference communications I questioned these examples (despite the fact that Poland, the most important candidate for the European Union in the first decade of the twenty-first century, has had annual growth rates close to 7% since 1995). On the other hand I pointed out what seems evident to me: the United States has been the main world engine for sustained economic growth in the 1990s.

Many economists fear that a recession affecting large parts of the world could evoke protectionist measures in some countries and retaliatory measures in others. This situation would reduce the interdependence created by globalization, along with the benefits it generates. But that way leads to worldwide economic disaster. Fortunately, the fear of a worldwide depression is not shared by world capital markets. As this book goes to press (summer 1998), stock exchanges are setting all-time highs, and there is widespread optimism about the economy of the United States. Nevertheless, as Robert Reich points out, it is possible that an accelerated global deflation will take place. Prices of raw materials and oil are still declining, interest rates do not decrease in proportion to inflation, American consumers sustain very high levels of debt, and Japan's economy is deflating; indeed, the decrease of demand in Japan is one of the factors that have pulled Asian economies down. [19]

---

[19] Robert Reich, Secretary of Labor in the Clinton Administration from 1993 to 1997 and now a professor at Brandeis, speaking to the Fellows of the Weatherhead Center for International Affairs, March 6th, 1998.

Conclusion

For what may seem like the nth time, I want to remind my readers that in 1998 it makes no sense to talk about the economy of a region, a country, or even a continent, without considering the global environment within which that economy operates. Chapter IV and V of this book, which examine the situation and problems of Europe and the benefits and disadvantages of the Monetary Union, try to observe this injunction. This global frame of reference accounts for whatever value my analysis may have. In the Darwinian capitalism which the world is going to live through in the next several decades, the success or failure of the European Union will depend on how the EU positions itself within the evolving global situation.

III. THE MONETARY UNION

Introduction

The EMU is Europe's latest response to a changing world. The European Union was conceived as an effort to overcome the continent's historic fragmentation -a disadvantageous position from which to compete for the future. The EMU, beyond all the technical detail, is intended to be another step towards the political union of Europe. It is also a significant step from an economic point of view. According to Commissioner Monti, the EMU was the missing ingredient in the development of the single European market.

The idea of creating a single currency is not new. In March 1971, the Council of Ministers of the Community approved the Werner Plan to establish a European Monetary Union by the early 1980's. A few months later the project was dropped; the members of the EEC thought that the exchange rate parities of European currencies would not survive the collapse of the Bretton Woods system. Adverse circumstances, as well as a lack of determination and will, buried the project until the emergence of Jacques Delors, the appropriate person to rescue it. In April 1987, a report of his friend Padoa-Schioppa convinced him that in a Europe with free movement and fixed interest rates, there was no place for separate and independent monetary policies. Ever since, Delors has made substantial efforts towards the establishment of the single currency, believing this achievement essential for Europe to compete with Japan and, specially, the United States.

Several circumstances favored this project: the economic bonanza in Europe, the success of the single market, and the ambitions of a number of politicians who saw an opportunity to leave their mark on history. Delors' most decisive step was convincing Helmut Kohl, who initially seemed opposed but became a fervent defender and even called the Euro a question of "war and peace". The single currency process culminated in the approval and signing of the Maastricht Treaty in December 1991. As is well known, the treaty created a timetable for putting the Monetary Union into effect, with a final deadline of January 1, 1999, and established five criteria to be fulfilled by every member country. These criteria have to do with inflation, interest-rate convergence, exchange rate stability, and fiscal discipline, requiring a budget deficit not exceeding 3% and a public debt not exceeding 60% of each country's GDP.

The difficulties of implementing the Treaty, including a "No" vote in the Danish referendum and the slim margin of approval in France, along with a recession in Europe during the period 1991-1993, slowed down the process of economic convergence. Widespread skepticism arose as to whether the Monetary Union would actually come about. At best, it seemed that the Union would have "two speeds", with only a few member countries as "ins" and the rest as "outs". Within the first group, though the United Kingdom and Denmark could opt out, the presence of Germany, France, Netherlands, Austria (not yet a member of the EU), Luxembourg, and perhaps Ireland was assured. Belgium presented a serious dilemma because its debt, the highest in the EU, exceeded 130% of GDP. On the other hand, the exclusion of Portugal, Italy, Greece and Spain appeared almost certain.

However, from the moment in 1993-94 when it became evident that France and Germany were determined that the Monetary Union be implemented by the planned date, all European governments initiated a frantic race to fulfill the five convergence criteria and not be left out. The EMU became the top political and economical priority among all countries of the European Union. In the autumn of 1996, the international financial markets also started to bet in favor of EMU and accelerated the convergence process by creating a "virtuous circle". The success of independent central banks in controlling inflation dramatically reduced interest rates as well as the cost of the public debt in the supposedly excluded countries. Thus, a paradox appeared: the "excludables" have managed to improve their economic growth and fulfill the Maastricht criteria partly through one-off privatizations and creative accounting, but also through a better numerator in the budget deficit ratio (higher tax income and lower public expenses) and a higher denominator (GDP). In contrast, Germany and France, the core of the Monetary Union, have passed the test by a very slim margin.

Finally, following the decision of the Council of Ministers of May 1998, the Monetary Union train will depart the following January with eleven passengers; out of fifteen members of the European Union, only the United Kingdom, Denmark, Sweden, and Greece will stay out, the first three by their own decision. Even Greece has improved so much that it seems very likely to be able to catch the Monetary Union train at its next stop (in 2001).

The EMU essentially became a commitment between France and Germany to exchange control of the monetary policy (until now exercised exclusively by the Bundesbank) for the achievement of political union. This union would allow Europe to hold its own in the world of economic blocs, that already seems near. It is in fact the fulfillment of a commitment undertaken in the Treaty of Rome, which spoke of progress towards "an ever closer union". The Monetary Union will be a milestone within this European integration process, entailing changes in political and economic structures as well as in the texture of everyday life.

The EMU has enthusiastic supporters and rabid detractors. Most of the supporters are in Europe; Americans are generally -though not unanimously– critical. Enthusiasts emphasize that the conservative economic policy dictated by Maastricht is intrinsically desirable and positive. The most outstanding cases of "fiscal restraint" (e.g., Ireland and Denmark) have been rewarded with higher economic growth. In addition, it is pointed out that the EMU will bring greater economic and political integration, as it will finally implement a real single market and will reduce transaction costs and eliminate uncertainty in exchange rates. Through other "spillovers", politicians hope that the EMU will help realize the project of a political union in Europe.

For the critics, the integration process seems to consume too much energy; the enormous effort involved in bringing the Monetary Union to its final stage could have been used to solve serious and dramatic problems like the expansion to the East, unemployment, and the general reform of economic systems which seem incapable of meeting future challenges. However, the main objection to the EMU is that it will not be able to fulfill the expectations it has created. As we will see in Chapter V, critics emphasize that the common currency is irreversible, and that therefore there is no solution for catastrophic scenarios. Obviously member countries will not be able to devalue their currency in order to become more competitive; they will lose control over their monetary policy, and even over their fiscal policy, because they will not be able to incur a budgetary deficit exceeding 3% of their GDP. The only possible reactions to adverse circumstances affecting only one country will be a decrease in prices and wages, or the mass exodus of its companies and labor force towards other countries. Nevertheless, most European leaders are convinced that the Monetary Union is a valuable project, trusting a process that has worked since the beginning of the Community: moving toward political union by means of economic cooperation.

Ralf Dahrendorf, former Commissioner of the European Union and well known for his "Euro-skepticism", predicted a year and a half ago that the Monetary Union would be irrelevant and would generate divisiveness among European countries[20]. Many other detractors, especially from the

---

[20]Paul-Henry Spaak Lecture, Center of International Affairs, Harvard University, October 2nd, 1996.

United States, agree. The most extreme case, as I note earlier, is Martin Feldstein's, who predicts that the Monetary Union will cause intra-European military conflict, and possibly even a war between the United States and Europe. I find Feldstein's pronouncements simplistic, Dahrendorf's somewhat more plausible. In any case, the seriousness of anti-"European" reactions following the implementation of EMU will depend laregely on the expectations that European electors have about it. As I will argue in Chapter VI, although EMU may not be the best thing for Europe, it is unlikely that it will turn into the catastrophe predicted by its detractors. The EMU's success or failure will depend on the success of failure of Europe's economy. Unfortunately, in some countries –Spain for example- the EMU has been presented as a panacea. At the very least, it is portrayed as a historic achievement and a reward for our efforts, leading the electorate to believe that the obstacles and sacrifices will have ended in May 1998, with the Council's decision to include Spain in the EMU. As the next chapter will argue, this is a dangerous illusion.

So far, the Treaty of Maastricht has not brought any progress toward political union except for monetary unification. The Intergovernmental Conference and the Treaty of Amsterdam have made it clear that there are some matters that states are unwilling to leave in the hands of European majorities, that every country maintains the veto right over issues considered of vital national interest, and that small countries are reluctant to lose influence in a future expansion. It is also evident that although the core countries will be able to make decisions related to the Monetary Union, unanimity will be required on fiscal matters, foreign policy and common security, justice, *Acquis Communautaire,* etc[21]. The two main pillars of the EU, Internal and Justice, and Common External and Security Policy, will continue to have a purely intergovernmental character.

Before Maastricht, economic union was thought to require significant progress towards political union. In fact, many of the main characters, preeminently Chancellor Kohl, worked for greater political union during the single currency negotiations. But it was not possible. Jacques Delors, considered the father of the treaty, was not fully satisfied with the product of his efforts, and thought that the time had not come to take a qualitative step towards federalism. Not only had it not arrived; it seemed as far away as ever.

The Treaty of Maastricht marked the apex of European centralized power, represented by the Commission, and also a serious warning to the national governments of what this entails. During the journey to the Euro, some country members were relegated to second fiddle. The Single European Act entailed new powers for the Commission, whose proposals were absolutely essential to achieve the single market; but country members would lose substantial control over the Community's agenda. In the end, there was no political union agreed on at Maastricht nor any step that would have implied a leap into the unknown. Since then, controlling of the decision-making process and limiting the initiatives of

---

[21]There is an an aspect of the Treaty of Amsterdam that should be taken into account: decisions in policy that hold certain difficulty are normally not taken until it is absolutely necessary. In this sense, time may judge differently the outcome of such Treaty.

the Commission have been matters of concern for all national governments. No country was prepared to take qualitative steps towards federation. And nowadays, as the disappointing Treaty of Amsterdam revealed, governments will not make a decision to further integration unless and until they absolutely have to. Yet a reform of the institutions of the European Union seems necessary since the present structure cannot stretch any further and is not geared to carry out the EU's enlargement and the inclusion of new members.

In Spain, there has been little internal debate about the advantage of the Monetary Union, except as to whether Spain would qualify. Even so, the Monetary Union has monopolized the attention and priorities of the last government of Felipe González and of José María Aznar, both supported by Convergencia i Unió and Jordi Pujol. In other European countries, especially those, like Germany, with the capacity to make decisions about the European political agenda, there has been total focus on the EMU, to the detriment of other issues. Even the notion that the conflict in the former Yugoslavia escalated as a result of inattention by Kohl and Mitterrand, who were too preoccupied with the Treaty of Maastricht, is all too plausible.

In Germany, where public opinion has been against replacing the Deutschmark with the Euro, many objections have risen against EMU. The president of the Bundesbank, Hans Tietmayer, warned in 1995 about the dangers of continuing with the EMU calendar towards monetary union without advancing simultaneously towards a political union, and hoped the project of the former would remain on hold in view of the evident lack of progress toward the latter. However, Kohl has shown unyielding determination; in October of 1995 he asserted that EMU was essential and that its implementation could mean the difference between war and peace in the twenty-first century.

The single currency has become the only major common project in Europe. To abandon it, in the opinion of many European politicians and civil servants, would have meant the end of the special Franco-German relation of the last twenty years.

IV. EUROPE: ASSETS AND LIABILITIES

Economic globalization means increased competition. Is Europe ready? A comparative analysis reveals an alarmingly long list of disadvantages at this moment of departure of the EMU train. A review of assets and liabilities is in order, since, in my experience, Europeans tend to overstimate their advantages and minimize their problems.

1. Assets

The European economy still holds important assets. The current population of the European Union, 380 million in a single market, still provides a considerable level of aggregate demand. It is true that since 1991 the economy of Europe has grown more slowly than that of the United States and that this, along with the currency realignment in 1997, has caused a decrease in Europe's share of the world economy. But its GDP of $7 trillion, provides a considerable level of aggregate demand. Europe's GDP continues to be slightly higher than that of the United States and is twice Japan's. To this fundamental advantage we may add others -some real, some dubious, some "double-edged".

- The recent increase in Europe's share of global trade. Indeed, the share of EU countries in global trade increased from 27.5% in 1986 to 33.4% in 1994, even before the incorporation of Austria, Sweden and Finland[22]. However, these growth figures include "intra-European" trade and therefore are not very significant.

- The increasing integration and specialization of European industry, which will probably increase economies of scale and efficiency.

- The trend toward dismantling European monopolies, privatizing state enterprises and liquidating unprofitable companies, resulting in greater competition, decreased subsidies, and increased productivity and competitiveness.

- The EU's privileged access to the growing markets of Eastern European countries (particularly advantageous for Germany). Although Europe is indeed well positioned to benefit from the development of its eastern neighbors, we must remember that these countries are going to increase the GDP of the EU by only 5% or so. We must not overestimate this possible "engine of growth".

- High education levels. Nevertheless, it is increasingly evident that the secondary education system is better in

[22] *Fast Forward,* Richard Carlson and Bruce Goldman, Harper Business, 1994, p. 67.

Asia, and that higher education is more practical and adapted to the labor market in the United States. [23]

- The strong public sector in Europe, where a much greater proportion of GNP passes through government hands and allows the undertaking of large infrastructure projects, unimaginable in other countries, where neither the private nor public sector can afford to finance them. Until now, the United States have been unable to undertake projects such as high-speed trains in the "northeastern corridor" between Washington, New York and Boston, or between Los Angeles and San Francisco, despite their almost certain profitability. Of course, the advantage of a financially powerful state is a two-edged. It allows the sinking of valuable resources in unprofitable projects such as the Franco-British Concorde (and others even worse) and at best, an important public sector takes competitiveness and dynamism away from the economy. On the other hand, the U.S. military has, in effect, subsidized many private companies through its research and development program.

- Europe's best asset is a much less unequal distribution of wealth and income than that of the United States. In the latter (and in the United Kingdom) the poorest 20% of the population receives less than 5% of total income,

---

[23] The TIMSS (Third International Mathematics adn Science Study), conducted in more than forty countries, whose results were published in 1997, proves the mediocrity of science education in most European countries, even in Germany, in relation to the Asian countries, with Singapore in first place (See *The Economist,* April 29, 1997, p. 21).

compared with more than 8% in Sweden, Netherlands, Luxembourg and Spain, and more than 7% in Germany and Belgium[24]. An unequal income distribution is not a good omen of future social harmony[25]. On the other hand, this relative egalitarianism has been achieved through redistributive policies that may be unsustainable in the long run, for fiscal reasons.

In sum, not all our assets have the same status: some are real, some are dubious, some are potential or hypothetical,

---

[24]World Bank, *World Development Report,* 1997, Table 22.

[25]Robert Reich is sharply critical of the prevailing triumphalism in the United States. Reich has presented a striking picture of the accelerated deterioration of wealth and income distribution in the United States, beginning in the late 1970s (and thus not, as many believe, the exclusive result of the neoliberal policies of Reagan and Bush). Although this trend halted, at least temporarily, in 1996, the wages of the poorest 40% of Americans have not increased in real terms since 1989, even though the economy has grown by more than 35% since then. Notwithstanding a remarkable decrease in unemployment (more than four million new jobs created annually by the U.S.economy), the number of American children living in poverty has increased by 20% since 1992, and there are still 41 million Americans who do not have medical insurance. The most interesting part of Reich's lecture was his analysis of reasons why Americans do not like to talk about this problem, which is similar to those that prevent Europeans from openly discussing the problems analyzed later on in this chapter.

Reich's greatest concern is that the United States is losing its tradition of equal oportunity. Until recently, upwards mobility was far more feasible, and any person, even if born in less favourable circumstances, was able to reach a high status with effort, education, and talent. For reasons that could fill another book, the deterioration and inequality of primary and secondary education in the United States, financed mostly by local property taxes, condemns the poorest, specially children born in urban ghettos, to remain in that underworld.

Reich offered a curious stadistic: in mid-March, the net worth of Bill Gates, founder and president of Microsoft, was estimated at $46 billion, higher than the aggregate net worth ($40 billion including houses, automobiles, savings, and other assets) of the poorest 100 million people in the United States. I have not been able to verify Reich's estimate; but if true, it provides further proof that globalization tends to increase inequalities.

and still others are double-edged (like the capacity of the public sector to invest in infrastructure).

TABLE 1			
EUROPEAN UNION ASSETS			
Real	**Potential**	**Double-edged**	**Doubtful**
Population	Eastern Europe	Public Sector	University Education
Dimension	Specialization		Social Protection
Current Income	Integration		Foreign Trade
Primary Education	More Competition		

2. Problems and Disadvantages

In *El Futuro de España* I wrote a paragraph that I now find naive: "Governments should be responsible for explaining the situation clearly to their electorates in order to increase the latter's understanding of the problems that affect them. Governments should initiate the necessary debates about these problems". [26]

---

[26] In a public discussion of *El Futuro de España* in Madrid, Miguel Ángel Fernández Ordoñez scolded me for my naivete in this respect. "Diego", he admonished, in a 'non-politically correct way', "politicians are like ladies and diplomats. If a lady says "no" she means "perhaps"; if she says"perhaps" she means "yes", and if she says "yes", she is not a lady. Conversely, the "yes" of a diplomat means "perhaps", "perhaps" means "no" ; and "no" means he is not a diplomat. A politician does not get involved with a controversial problem; if he does, he will deal with it vaguely and superficially; if he deals with it concretely and in depth, he is not a politician."

TABLE 2				
EUROPE'S PROBLEMS				
Vision	**Structure**	**Demographic**	**Governance**	**Political**
Shortsightedness	Unemployment	Public Health	Divergences	Internal Conflicts
Endogamy	CAP	Pensions	Leadership	Common Foreign Policy
Lack of Self-criticism	Costs			Maghreb: Regional conflicts
Destructiveness	Incentives			
	Dynamism			
	Budget Balance			
	Dependence			
	Inferior Technology			
	German Engine			

This chapter will analyze each of these problems and will reach an alarming conclusion: the EMU will not resolve any of them and may even pose an additional obstacle to solving them.

(a) Vision.

The first problem, applicable to Europe and especially to Spain, is a lack of vision. Europeans are generally (i) oriented toward the short-run, (ii) endogamic, (iii) reluctant to see their own problems and liable to overestimate their abilities, and (iv) prone to expending far too much energy in sterile internal disputes.

(i)   INABILITY TO THINK MEDIUM- AND LONG- TERM. Europeans lack long-term vision. Politicians adopt a philosophy of "après moi le deluge": addressing thorny problems may lose them votes and perhaps even bail out political rivals. The private sector also displays this lack of vision. Perhaps because of the failure of past five-year plans, forecasts rarely go further than the budget for the current fiscal year.

This shortsightedness also applies to the EMU. Literature on how it may work and what problems it may encounter has, until recently, been remarkably scarce. Potential problems, such as "asymmetric shocks" –economic crises affecting one member of the EMU and not the others- or the elimination of a lender of last resort to give stability to the banking system, have not been analyzed. The EMU has done nothing to correct the emphasis on short-term measures or the priority of short- over medium- term considerations. On the contrary, the mad rush toward EMU imposed by Maastricht has prevent countries from tackling such problems as pension reform, which requires measures costly in the short run but indispensable in the long run.

(ii) ENDOGAMY. It is true that Americans tend to be isolationist and to ignore the rest of the world. However, we Europeans are inward-looking at precisely the moment in which it is more necessary than ever before to look outwards. Globalization requires outward-looking and open economies; only external competitiveness guarantees internal competitiveness. We have yet to recognize that, despite the Asian crisis, the Pacific may be replacing the Atlantic as the world's center of gravity, and Europe may find itself on the periphery.

This judgement is not mine alone. Ever since I moved to United States in 1994 I have been hearing it from ministers and high officials, Asian colleagues, American and European businessmen, and the U.S. academic community attentive to developments in Europe. Ralf Dahrendorf, ex-Commissioner of the European Union, has denounced endogamy as one of worst ills of Europe[27]. Jeffrey Sachs has warned that "the EMU has monopolized the attention of Europeans to the detriment of dealing with urgent structural problems and of the constructive role that Europe should have played in the world recently".[28]

---

[27] Ralf Dahrendorf, *Paul Henri Spaak Annual Lecture,* delivered October 2, 1996, and published by the Weatherhead Center for International Affairs, Harvard University, 1996.
[28] Lecture, Cambridge, MA, January 27, 1998.

(iii) Reluctance to acknowledge our own problems. We may be looking inward, but we are not seeing clearly. In Spain, we still refuse to acknowledge the unsustainability of our pension system, pretending that the Pact of Toledo will solve everything. In France, many people actually believed Jospin's pre-election promises regarding employment creation. Many French, Italian and Spanish people seem to think that enacting a 35-hour work week without salary cuts will create jobs.

(iv) Sterile controversies. Europeans too often create needless controversy and polarization. Few leaders even try to evoke belief in a common project. In some countries, voters are increasingly positioning themselves on the extremes of the political spectrum. The media have not played a constructive role, and politicians have been unnecessarily acrimonious. Any leader who actually tries to lead is immediately criticized. [29]

These vision problems are very serious. Far from correcting them, the EMU has diverted Europeans' attention, preventing them from finding solutions to real problems and embarking on more profitable and constructive projects.

---

[29] Jimena Menéndez Pidal, a wise former teacher, used to ask us students to imagine an American, a European, and a Spaniard trying to climb up a tree towards a prize. The American's compatriots would encouraging him and push him up the tree. The European's would observe in silence. The Spaniard's would pull him down by his trousers until he fell.

(b) Economic Structure

1. UNEMPLOYMENT in Europe is much higher than in United States or Japan, and is perceived by most Europeans as our main problem. Though in some countries unemployment rates are moderate (6% in United Kingdom and the Netherlands, 7% in Austria, Denmark and Portugal), in most countries they are above 10% (11.3% in Germany, 12.6% in France, 12.2% in Italy, 12.8% in Belgium, 15% in Finland and almost 20% in Spain). The European Union average is around 11%.

Although Spain is, along with United Kingdom, the only European country where official unemployment has decreased (from 24% in 1994 to 19.6% in 1998) our data on unemployment are not reliable. On the one hand, they do not take into account the informal economy; many analysts believe that official figures overestimate Spanish unemployment because many of the unemployed do have jobs but are paid in cash. On the other hand, there are several reasons to believe that the official figures underestimate the magnitude of unemployment in Spain:

- Our ratio of university students to total population is the highest in Europe, but this is the result of deliberately low standards: i.e. letting bad students go out into a slack labor market would, it is thought, aggravate an already serious social problem. Even so, our unemployment rate among 18-25 year-olds is already, at 40%, the highest in the European Union.

- Our labor force as a percentage of the working-age population (59%) is, with Italy, the lowest in Europe, where the average is 68%. This could betoken a submerged economy, but our unemployment rate would probably be much higher if that differential of 9% were added to the ratio's numerator and denominator. [30]

• Spain ranks last in Europe in the proportion of employed among its working-age population. More than half of Spanish working-age people (51.9%) do not have a job. [31]

• "Shadow unemployment", the difference between the official number of employed and the number that would exist assuming labor market liberalization and the rationalization of public administration, is much higher than in United States, Canada, and other countries. I will return to this point when discussing state dependency.

Although Spain's position is the worst in the EU, unemployment is a fairly general problem. About fifteen years ago, when European economies were flourishing, no one spoke of unemployment as a structural problem. It was assumed that growth would take care of unemployment. This might have been true had governments simply removed barriers to employment and allowed the private sector to do the rest. Instead, European governments did the opposite; they engaged in even greater economic activity, reaching

---

[30] *El Futuro de España* (pg. 233-266) dedicates a chapter to the unemployment problem in Spain.

[31] See Employment Outlook, (OECD, July, 1997).

around 50% of GNP of most countries of the European Union. As a result, after the economic cycle peaked, unemployment reached unacceptable rates. Structural unemployment, one that does not cure by a return of good times, is still growing in most of the EU, to the point that unemployment is considered the main European problem today.

In the United States unemployment has decreased to 4.5%, a level which most economists recently believed was incompatible with stable inflation. In 1997 average unemployment in Europe exceeded 11%. Unemployment among those under 25 has reached 21.3%, and is particularly dramatic in Italy (33.7%), Finland (37.2%), and Spain (40.3%). Gary Becker[32] finds it frightening that in Western Europe the number of jobs in the private sector has not increased since 1965. Between 1970 and 1998, the US has generated more than forty-five million jobs. The European Union has created 9 million: one million in the private sector and the other eight in the public sector.[33]

Even more significant than the unemployment rate –in which many who want to work are not counted– is the employment/population ratio. According to the last OECD report, the 1996 ratio for the European Union was 59.1%, somewhat less than in 1983. In Japan it was 74.6%, up from 71.0% in 1983; and in the U.S., it was 75%, up from 68.% in 1983[34]. Inside the European Union, according to the same report, employment ratios vary substantially, from 71% in

---

[32] Op. cit.

[33] "EU summit urged to agree on targets for training jobless" (Lionel Barber in Brussels, *Financial Times,* September 4, 1997).

[34] Employment Outlook, (OECD, July, 1997).

the UK to 64 % in Germany (where it has worsened during the last year), 59.6% in France, 51% in Italy and 48.1% for Spain, which is the only industrialized country where there are more working-age people without a job than with one.

It is also significant to note that the employment ratio in the European Union for the population in the 55-64 age-bracket has decreased from 40.7% in 1983 to 35.1% in 1996, while in the United States it increased from 54.5% to 57.9% and the employment/population rate rose from 51.4% to 55.9%. The case of Japan is even more remarkable: the employment ratio in the 55-64 age bracket was 61.3% in 1983 and 63.6% in 1996.

In 1996, long-lasting unemployment, (i.e., more than twelve months) in the United States was only 9.6% of total unemployment. In France it was 39.5%, in Germany 48.3% (1995 data), in the Netherlands 49% and more than 50% and in other EU countries such as Portugal, Spain, Ireland and Italy, where it reached 65.5%.

This leads us to two main conclusions. The first is that changes in the world since the 1970s have affected mainly the European labor market. The second is that globalization and technology changes pose threats but also opportunities. The example of the United States shows how accepting change as an opportunity and a culture of innovation as something to be proud of, can lead to a period of unprecedented economic growth with low inflation, low unemployment levels and virtually no long-term unemployment.

The same period has brought unemployment and a sluggish economy to Europe. There is no single cause for this, but among the causes are surely the extreme rigidity of

European labor markets [35], the state's asphyxiation of private initiative, and a persistent incapacity to adapt. Europe lacks the political will to make the necessary sacrifices to become dynamic and competitive. There is no miracle nor immediate solution for unemployment in Europe. Alternative policies to fight unemployment involving medicines such as the ones undertaken by Holland for many years, the so-called "proactive strategy", simply result in a tremendous shadow unemployment, underlining the fact that there are no substitute for flexible labor markets.

Robert Reich has pointed out the essential conditions for generating employment. According to Reich, these conditions are like the three legs of a stool:

(a) The first is complete flexibility in the labor market with freedom to hire and fire (the latter term is taboo in Europe), and wage flexibility moderated only by a minimum wage, complemented with a "tax credit for the employed."

(b) The second is that the current **security nets** (unemployment insurance) be replaced by a **springboard** system: substantial investment by government and the private sector in education and fast retraining, along with a public or private network of placement agencies that allows individuals to find another job quickly

---

[35] The World Economic Outlook issued by the IMF on April 11, 1998 refers to the rigidity of the European labor markets as the "Achylles heel of EMU" (page 26). The term was used repeatedly by Flemming Larsen, Deputy Director of the Research Department of the IMF, in his presentation of the report broadcast by C-SPAN on April 17, 1998.

after losing a former one, and that increases their adaptability to labor-market demand;

(c) Proper fiscal policy to maintain the aggregate demand level necessary for generating jobs.

According to Reich, United States deserves an A+ for its labor flexibility, a C for its **springboard** (with a D for a primary education system which does not allow the population of the urban ghettos to break out of their vicious circle and move upwards in society), and a B in macroeconomic management, though he is concerned about present deflationary forces and that failure of the Federal Reserve to lower interest rates. If one applied grades to Europe, it would have a D - or rather an F- in both labor flexibility and springboard system, thereby making macroeconomic management irrelevant to generating employment.

The victims of this situation are the unemployed. In recent years, both unions and governments have hoisted the employment flag; but the fact is, the former have only defended the privileges of those who already have a job[36], and the latter have found no solutions other than to provide generous unemployment compensation. These subsidies have been an important support for the unemployed and are, along with family solidarity, the reason that European countries with high unemployment have not suffered serious social disturbances. Relatively equal income distribution and the resulting social peace are genuine assets. We must ask ourselves,

---

[36] As Franco Modigliani, Nobel laureate in Economics, has pointed out in relation to Spain.

however, whether they are being achieved by sacrificing the prospects of a whole generation, and whether they are financially sustainable in the long run.

The EMU will not solve or even improve the unemployment problem in Europe. On the contrary, recent research suggests that it may aggravate the problem [37]. Most academic specialists in the United States agree that the European Central Bank will have to undertake strict monetary policies, which will be deflationary and will negatively affect employment. While I believe that interest rates do not influence employment as much as others variables, it is clear that the EMU will not significantly improve the situation.

2. THE COMMON AGRICULTURE POLICY (CAP) will not be able to survive the EU's expansion eastward. The CAP is an economic aberration that forces Europeans to pay excessive prices for food and provides subsidies to a small agricultural sector, mainly for not producing. It fosters corruption, distorts resource allocation, promotes a culture of subsidy dependence, and harms the many to benefit the few. (In fact, the CAP rewards small farmers less than rich ones). Furthermore, CAP hurts the EU's image and foreign relations by preventing poor regions, like the North African countries, from selling their only competitive resources. The same is true in not-so-poor countries, like those in Central and Eastern Europe.

The CAP must be reformed. Besides being irrational and unfair, the CAP will be rendered unsustainable by the EU's

---

[37] David Cameron: *European Union and Unemployment,* Conference at the Center of European Studies, Harvard University, February 13, 1998.

expansion to the East. CAP reform is also necessary in order for the EU to participate in the WTO negotiations in 1999, where liberalization of financial services and agriculture will be on the agenda. European agricultural prices should approach world prices, and export subsidies should no longer be allowed.

The reform proposals included in the Agenda 2000 are far from satisfactory. Although the number of farmers is declining and the percentage of the EU's population employed in agriculture has decreased from 30% to less than 6%, farmers still have considerable political power and few governments dare to attack their privileges, no matter how unfair. As a Commission official said recently: "One can guess what the agriculture ministers are going to say in their European encounters, because it differs little from what agricultural leaders have been saying the previous week"[38]. Perhaps this is the reason why the agriculture reforms proposed by Commissioner Fischler have so far not been substantial.

It is plausible that, under the pressures from the EMU and the World Trade Organization, reforms will be undertaken. However, the Common Agriculture Policy is one of the mainstays of the Union, and no country seems ready to abandon it or seriously reform it. This means that new countries entering the European Union will have to face complex negotiations; and that the rest of the world will have to deal with Europe's continued effort to protect agriculture, as well as many dying industries, rather than seek opportunities in more promising sectors.

---

[38] See "The Great Survivor", Michael Smith, *Financial Times,* Monday, November 3, 1997.

The CAP may be a minor problem compared with others discussed in this long chapter, which aims to remind readers of the serious problems that cloud Europe's future while the EMU monopolizes the attention of governments, media, and the public. Europeans are not alone, of course, in overprotecting their agriculture: Japan produces its own rice at extremely high cost, and the United States supports artificially high sugar prices, seriously harming the economic development of Caribbean and Central American countries. Even so, it is important that Europe recognize and solve this problem, and the EMU will do nothing to help.

3. PRODUCTION COSTS IN EUROPE ARE THE HIGHEST IN THE WORLD FOR MANY REASONS. [39]

- labor costs, even net of payroll taxes designated to cover pensions, are the highest in the world; Germany's are even higher than Japan's;

- energy costs are much higher (by 50%) than in the United States: gasoline, for example, is three times more expensive in Europe;

- long-distance telephone calls are three times more expensive; Internet connections cost almost double; the

---

[39] An article in *Financial Times,* "Workers pay for Europe's rigidities" (Emma Tucker, February 13, 1998) analyzes a comprehensive study on competitiveness of the EU *(Benchmarking Europe's Competitiviness: from Analysis to Action de UNICE).* This study reveals a EU loaded with high non-wage costs, short working hours, regulatory barriers and swollen public sectors. According to George Jacobs, chairman of Unice group for competitiviness, the reaction needed for employment generation is to reduce non-wage labor costs, which amount to 80% of total wage costs in the EMU and less than 40% in USA.

restriction of commercial hours reduces options for consumers and also reduces employment;

- real estate is much more expensive in Europe; as many in the financial sector have pointed out, overpriced land is a sign of poor economic health; [40]

- the overvaluation of land is a major risk for financial systems and domestic economies: a sharp drop in prices may produce financial crisis; it is prudent to bear in mind that the United States assimilated and overcame such crisis in the 1980s, that Asia is currently undergoing it, and that Europe's crisis has not yet arrived.

It is true that the credibility of the EMU project among international financial markets has helped reduce financial costs for companies and governments, specially for countries with weak economies. However, for all other costs of production, unless the European Central Bank follows a lax monetary policy that weakens the Euro (a very improbable assumption), it appears that the EMU will not remove this key obstacle for the competitiveness of Europe in the future, and may even aggravate it.

4. THE INCENTIVE TO CREATE COMPANIES in Europe is much lower, and the obstacles much greater, than in other industrialized countries. Entrepreneurship in Europe carries less social prestige and more risks than in other parts of the

---

[40] Peter Aldrich, Conference on the EMU organized in Harvard by the WCFIA and CES, January 27th, 1998.

world. Furthermore, personal and business taxes are so high that many people considerer abandoning Europe as their fiscal residence. The warning of the Gorbachev Foundation about the loss of sovereignty of countries and the permeability of frontiers appears justified; in the medium-term future, multinational companies with headquarters in Europe will look for more favorable fiscal jurisdictions.

There are wide variances within Europe. In Spain, for many years, it has been and still is more profitable and less risky to invest in real estate than in the productive sectors. It is possible that the Monetary Union will highlight the absurdity of the differences in land and real estate prices among member countries, but it is not likely that it will do much about the lack of incentives to create enterprises in Europe.

The first problem a potential entrepreneur faces is the above-mentioned high costs of production. The second is government protection of sectors such as telecommunications, agriculture and small business. The result is that telephone calls are three times more expensive in Europe than in the United States, travel is substantially more expensive, and so is energy, e.g., petroleum and electricity. The protection of small retailers is supposed to be accomplished by putting limits on shopping malls, large-scale retailing and hours of operation. In fact, however, not only are small shop owners not protected, they are worse off. Limiting hours makes it more difficult for them to compete with big retailers; restrictions prevent them from specializing; labor rigidity renders them unable to hire employees at lower costs, etc. Restrictive zoning increases the price of land in almost all countries of the Union, although in some of them, such as Spain, there are plenty of buildings left unoccupied.

There is another type of barriers to innovation. In the course of its research on production, productivity and employment, the McKinsey Global Institute identified important obstacles in financial services sectors in countries where there are fewer instruments than in the United States and where innovations only arrive after many years. According to McKinsey, "restriction in service markets is probably the most important factor when it comes to explaining differences of employment from one country to another". These restrictions are regulations that prevent the adoption of competitive production processes and hinder innovation in products and services; for example, zoning laws, minimum-distance rules, or the lack of such financial products as private pension funds or risk-capital.[41]

Regulations and standards. A further disincentive to create new companies is over-regulation, a factor examined in greater detail later on. Entrepreneurs must frequently pay attention to so many administrative details that their activity becomes very expensive. As a result, anyone starting a new business faces tremendous obstacles. As former Chancellor Helmut Schmidt affirmed recently, in Germany the most daring entrepreneur "has to overcome the nuisance of about 5,000 pages of sometimes archaic legal texts"[42]. The envi-

---

[41] Comparative Study on Employment in four European Countries, McKinsey Global Institute, 1996.

[42] *Germany edges toward deregulation.* (Thomas Kau, Survey; Social Europe, *European Voice,* April 30 - May 6, 1997).

ronment created in this way is anything but favorable for enterprise creation. Even if it makes transnational operations easier by removing uncertainties about exchange rates, it is difficult to see how the Monetary Union is going to reduce regulatory barriers for entrepreneurs and make the development of new companies less complicated.

5. THE LACK OF DYNAMISM of European companies compared with American or Asian ones is a result of our endogamy, our excessively theoretical education, the bureaucratic obstacles encountered by enterprises, and the general interventionism and over-regulation of the private sector by governments. The over-regulation and excessive reporting requirements that throttle entrepreneurs in Europe affects almost all aspects of a company's operations. I have already mentioned the rigidity of labor markets. Other overburdened areas are risk-capital, land and buildings, energy, and telecommunications, in addition to complex reporting rules on transaction and income taxes. In some cases, regulatory en-thusiasm is a result of a misguided concern for the welfare of workers or for protecting economic sectors and companies which used to be considered "in the national interest" but are no longer economically viable. In other cases, government agencies are merely trying to justify their own existence by finding new areas in which their intervention is necessary to "protect the citizens".

It is not surprising that fewer jobs are created in Europe than in the United States. European entrepreneurs are hobbled by red tape. In a recent opinion poll, businessmen wanted three things from their governments: less bureaucracy, a more flexible labor market, and fewer social costs that tax employment[43]. As one of those interviewed stated, "governments should 'modernize' and globalize institutions which are relevant for businesses".

Regarding the **labor market,** European governments are still too concerned about protecting workers. It often appears undesirable for an entrepreneur to hire anyone because of the high costs incurred if their company has to close down or to move; rigid regulations prevent them from using their resources efficiently. This puts the brakes on the creation of new enterprises, and also affects businesses and companies already established; even in good economic times they may fear to hire anyone. "Experiences shows us that, when dismissal costs are low, private companies voluntarily risk hiring a greater number of workers".[44]

Furthermore, officially-mandated employment options, such as part-time or temporary work or work at home, must be offered and in many cases are hedged about with unrealistic rules. It is significant, for example, to observe the differences in the proportion of part-time workers in some European countries, such as the Netherlands and Great Britain, and others, such as France or Germany, even standardizing definitions to cover all those who work less than 30 hours a week.[45]

Labor mobility is low. As if the rigidity of national labor regulations and family and language ties were not enough, there are other difficulties for workers seeking to move from

---

[43]*Business environment, Call to reduce the red tape.* (Poll: Europe's most respected companies. Tony Jackson, *Financial Times,* September 24, 1997).

[44]Phelps, Edmund S. *Restore competitive capitalism. (El País.* Wednesday, October 1, 1997).

[45]See OECD, *Employment Outlook,* July 1997, page 178.

one country of the Union to another: in particular, inadequate legislation concerning unified retirement benefits and unemployment compensation. Pension system privatization and a Social Security system with transportable unemployment benefits would make mobility easier.[46]

6. The difficulty of balancing the budget with real and not cosmetic measures (e.g. privatizations, which can only be done once) bump against the ceiling of an already excessive fiscal pressure, as well as against the trends towards higher public expenditure.

The EU's Council of Ministers seems to have decided to not apply the Maastricht requirement that public debt be under 60% of GDP. The reasons for ignoring this criteria may be partly economic (interest rates and therefore debt service costs are lower in 1998 than they were in 1991 when the Treaty was signed) and partly political (getting around Belgium's debt of 123% of GDP, the highest in Europe). It would have been very difficult to leave Belgium (where the Commission has its headquarters) out of the Monetary Union, especially considering its monetary union with Luxembourg. However, the reasons that led the signers of the Treaty of Maastricht to include the debt criteria are still in force. For Belgium and Italy, two countries whose debt far exceeds their GDP, it will be very difficult to keep a budget deficit under 3% if interest rates increase.[47]

---

[46]Razin, Assaf / Yen, Chi-Wa. *Labour Mobility and Fiscal Coordination.* NBER Working Paper N° 5433. National Bureau of Economic Research, Cambridge (MA) January, 1996.

[47]Diego Hidalgo, *The European Monetary Union: creating "first" and "second class citizens"* in the EU. DFC Spotlight, Spring, 1997.

The EMU's Stability Pact imposed by Germany to convince its citizens that their currency will not lose purchasing power when replaced by the Euro, inflicts severe fines on countries running deficits higher than 3% of GDP. Hence, this is the only European problem that we are examining of which the Monetary Union may contribute to the solution. At least it would create pressure to lower the public expenditures of member countries.

There are, however, widespread doubts about the enforceability of the Stability Pact. It is also doubtful that states will be able to balance their budgets, given the rising pressure on spending likely to result from growing unemployment, the increasing liabilities of pension systems, and the costs of expanding the European Union to Eastern European countries. Although there is no doubt that the Monetary Union has brought about some degree of fiscal restraint among candidate countries, I am skeptical about the prospects of any additional benefits once it starts.

7. DEPENDENCY ON THE STATE, particularly unfortunate in an era of Darwinian capitalism, affects a much higher proportion of the population in Europe than anywhere else. This dependent population includes students, the unemployed, pensioners, and civil servants. Spain leads Europe in the proportion of university students, unemployed, and public pensioners. The number of civil servants in Spain has doubled in the last fifteen years. The high proportion of "tenured" civil servants to the total employed population is a serious problem throughout Europe; only the United Kingdom has addressed it, though Italy has announced a gradual reform to begin in the near future.

United States has a tradition of citizens independence and of deep mistrust for centralized authority. Only since the Great Depression of the 1930s have a large number of Americans been forced to depend on the government. The need for a strong government continued throughout the rest of the century because the country went through several crises: World War II in the Forties, The Korean War in the Fifties, Vietnam in the Sixties and early Seventies, the Cold War with the Soviet Union, besides other political and economic crises such as Watergate, Irangate, and the bailout of savings and loan associations. Since the end of the Cold War, the trend has been towards a reduction of government and a devolution of responsibility to individuals. In Europe, however, the state continues to be held responsible for every misfortune and difficulty experienced by citizens.

The development of the Monetary Union is not going to change this mentality; at most, governments will divert responsibility of crises to the European Central Bank, thus promoting anti-European feelings.

8. THE TECHNOLOGICAL INFERIORITY of Europe condemns us to play a secondary role, or even no role, in several growth sectors, where it will not be easy to recover market positions lost in the last few decades. Some Europeans dispute this and argue that a few European small enterprises have been able to achieve positions of technological leadership in some advanced industries; the fact is that most of these enterprises initiated by Europeans have later moved to the United States because of Europe's unfavorable business environment and regulations.

Although public expenditure is much higher in Europe than in United States, Europeans have not been able to produce high-yielding research and development in advanced technologies. As a result, Europe lags behind in the most promising sectors: biotechnology, new materials, and especially microprocessors, hardware and software. No company like Intel, Microsoft, or even Apple, has been created in Europe in the last thirty years, and no European company is among the world leader in any of these sectors. The only advanced sectors where Europe is competitive are high-speed trains and telecommunications equipment; the other advanced sector with a European presence is the aerospace industry, but without subsidies the Airbus consortium would have great difficulty competing with Boeing.

The first reason for this lag lies in specialized capital markets. One of the important assets American businessmen count on are venture-capital companies specializing in the provision of capital to new enterprises; these also fulfill a screening function, distinguishing viable ventures from those likely to fail. This venture-capital sector has been vital to creating new technologies companies in the U.S. and explains in part why Europe is far behind[48]. In 1994, 65% of the investment of risk-capital companies in the U.S. was directed towards new technology companies (50% of them in California and Massachusetts), while in Europe the percentage of already much smaller funds was only 15% (OECD, 1996).[49]

---

[48] *United States, 1997.* OECD Economic Surveys, Paris, December, 1997.

[49] One of my best friends, a classmate at Harvard Business School during 1966-68, is Frank Caufield, founder partner of Kleiner, Perkins, Caufield & Byers, the venture-

Another important factor in the lag could be labor market rigidities, confirming that almost all structural economic problems in Europe are interrelated. Gilles Saint-Paul has an interesting theory that is relevant here. According to him, "the rigidity of the European labor markets may have a much more harmful –and less studied– effect on long-term productivity through its influence on international specialization and innovation"[50]. To prove it, Saint-Paul elaborates a model which analyzes consequences -especially firing costs- that labor market institutions have on R&D and on international specialization. The basic idea is that to prevent dismissal compensation costs, a country with a rigid labor market will tend to produce goods with a relatively stable demand and which are at an advanced stage of their life cycle, that is, it will concentrate in the so-called "mature" industries.

It seems clear that in the technology race, Europe is behind. R&D as a percentage of GDP is about 20% higher in the U.S. and Japan than in Europe. It is also evident that the U.S. and Japan are considerably better than Europe in producing and exporting high technology products." At the Economic Forum in Davos in February 1997, Bill Gates scolded European businessmen for their technological infe-

capital company in United States without which big companies such as Lotus or Netscape couldn't have emerged. Frank, who speaks Spanish like a native, received telephone calls in 1983 from leaders of PSOE in Spain asking him to give advice the government on promotion of new technologies and establishment of venture-capital companies. Despite his availability, the Spanish government soon lost interest in an exploration that might have been very profitable for the country.

[50]Giles Saint-Paul, *Employment Protection, International Specialization and Innovation*. IMF Working Paper, WP/96/16. International Monetary Fund, February, 1996.

riority. He said he was shocked to discover Europe's scarce use of software[51]. Microsoft is one of the best-known companies in Europe, and in recent years there has been a considerable increase in the use of Internet and email by Europeans, with a resulting gradual disappearance of "computer illiteracy" even among the aging population. This is a favorable evolution for Europe. Although this technological advance in consumption does not by itself entail progress in production capabilities, it does contribute to the creation of small companies and employment in the computer service sector, and improves our education system and the prospects of important future discoveries or developments. Nevertheless, it is useful to underline once more our technological inferiority in these sectors as well as in the entertainment and leisure, computer, and audio sectors, to remember that this will constrain Europe's leadership in the 21st century, and to emphasize that this problem is not going to be solved or even improved by the Monetary Union.

9. THE GERMAN GROWTH-ENGINE is so heavily burdened by the costly absorption of East Germany that it has hardly been able to fulfill the Maastricht criteria. The Monetary Union is not going to help solve this problem.

More than two years ago, Germany's capacity to "pull the European train" was already seriously endangered. As I wrote at the end of 1995, "the German issue should be submitted to scrutiny. There are many Spaniards who think that Germany's leadership will be a decisive factor as Europe's

---

[51] *Profile: Microsoft. The company feared the most.* (Survey: Europe's most respected companies. Louise Kehoe. *Financial Times,* September 24, 1997).

engine of growth during the 21st century. The power and dynamism of German economy has become a common theme, and until recently anybody who affirmed that Germany could lose its international competitiveness in automobiles, machinery, and chemical products, without acquiring them in new technologies in which it lags behind, was not taken seriously. This competitiveness is threatened by very high taxes, pensions and one of the most expensive workforces in the world".[52]

According to the index of *The Economist's* Intelligence Unit, which compares relative costs of doing business in twenty-seven advanced countries, Germany is the most expensive of all. The index compiles statistics on wage and fixed costs, air transport, subsistence, corporate taxes, perceived levels of corruption, bureaucratic procedures, office and industrial rent, and road transport. Germany is the most expensive country, mainly because of its high level of basic wages[53]. Furthermore, to launch an enterprise in Germany is tremendously complicated. As I noted earlier, former German Chancellor Helmut Schmidt remarked a few months ago that anyone who wanted to start a new business in Germany was faced with the task of reading nearly 5,000 pages of archaic legal texts[54]. The incredible complexity of the statutory system drives entrepreneurs to hire costly groups of experts to assess the possible consequences of every decision, thereby slowing foreign investment in

---

[52] *El Futuro de España,* page 186.

[53] "Economic Indicators: Business Costs": *(The Economist,* January 24, 1998, page 116).

[54] *Germany edges towards deregulation.* (Thomas Klau. Survey: Social Europe. European Voice, April 30-May 6, 1997).

Germany, encouraging German companies to invest outside the country, and forcing many potential entrepreneurs to give up and choose the convenience of a salaried job.

This does not mean that the future of German industry is totally dim. Many companies manage to adapt to this hostile framework through innovations, external advice, or relocation. As Hans-Olaf Henkel, leader of the Federation of German Industry (BDI), observes: "Many of the most successful German companies achieve success mainly because they leave Germany, reestablishing their residence in countries where workers earn less or are more flexible. Some of the biggest German industries, such as Bayer, the chemical giant, are now achieving most of their profits in foreign countries"[55]. The problem lies with small -and medium- size companies that cannot relocate in foreign countries, or with those which never get to exist because there is no proper environment for them. For example, there are "100-year-old laws which restrain hiring academics in companies, and this means constraining the relation between universities and businesses, which should be one of the most important and fertile points in the modern economy. Although there are links in Germany, for example, between engineering colleges and big industries, these, in the past, have been less entrepreneurial"[56]. Restrictions go even further, from business hours to the length of the work week to annual vacations, which are the longest in the developed world. It is not surprising that entrepreneurs such as Henkel sponsor studies like "Vision of an attractive Germany", which shows

---

[55] Action man, *The Economist*, September 13, 1997. pg. 73.
[56] German Lessons, *The Economist*, October 18, 1997. pg. 89.

Germans "how their country could be in the year 2010 if they were only prepared to adapt themselves to the times". Their Germany would be remarkably different from the current one: mobile, flexible, efficient in energy consumption, and with less Government.

Perhaps Germany can break out of this vicious circle of government interventionism and become Europe's growth engine once more. This, however, will be a long process. It is important to stress that the Monetary Union will not solve Germany's problems, nor will it help create new growth "engines" to replace Germany.

(c) Demographic Problems

Next to unemployment and limited opportunities for job creation, the rapid aging of the population is the most urgent-to-resolve question mark in Europe's future. The inversion of the population pyramid is going to require so many resources that, unless stringent measures are taken soon, many European governments will be overwhelmed.

The consequences of an aging population include not only an increase in health-care expenses, but also, potentially, the bankruptcy of our pension systems. Health care and old-age pensions already constitute the two most important items in European national budgets; their growth could lead to the insolvency of European states, particularly because of the nature of the present pay-as-you-go pension systems.

The EMU not only will not solve these problems; it is certain to aggravate them, because the obligation to comply with the Maastricht criteria before 1998 and the Stability Pact after this year excludes any solution which though relieving budgetary expenses in the medium and long term, increase them in the short term. This is the case of the transition from our pay-as-you-go system to a capitalized one, a viable and needed alternative but out of the question if we want to keep our annual deficit below 3% of GDP in each of the next few years.

Japan's demographic evolution resembles Europe's, and will likely bring Japan similar problems. The U.S. is in a much more favorable position, to the benefit of its international competitiveness.

DEMOGRAPHICS

Despite the increases in life expectancy in the EU countries, birth rates have fallen so much that total European population is stagnant and about to decrease. Expected annual population increases in the EU will fall from 0.5% this decade to 0.0% in 2020, and in Germany, Italy and Spain total population is expected to start decreasing by 2010. In contrast, the percentage of the population 65 and over is expected to increase dramatically, reflecting higher fertility rates in the post-World War II period as well as advances in nutrition and medicine. While in 1965 people over 64 represented only 9.7% of total population, by 2000 they will have increased to 14.7% and by 2030 it will be over 23%. The over-74 share in total population will almost double, from 6% in 1990 to 11% in 2030. The increases of life expectancy in most population projections is between 4 and 5 years, to 80-82 years[57]. Many specialists assert that life expectancies could be considerably higher.

It follows from all this that the working-age population will decrease at a considerably faster rate than total population. After 2020 working-age population will decrease in all of OECD's Europe except Ireland. Ten years later, this population will have fallen by 4.5% from its highest point, expected in 2005, in the OECD as a whole. But this fall will be much higher in European countries; in Germany it will be 24%, while it will reach 18% in Italy and 15% in the Netherlands and Spain. The ratio of the population over 65 to the working age population will almost double between 1990 and 2030, passing from 19% to 37% for the OECD as a whole, and well above 40% in several European countries, such as Germany and Italy.

Even under conditions of full employment, this demographic evolution would create difficult problems; unemployment converts it into a looming disaster. If we take into account the fact that only 59 out of every 100 people of working age were employed in 1996, the ratios presented above become even more alarming. Every worker would have to support one retired person, in addition to children, students and the unemployed. And this does not take into account the large number of workers in the public sector, who are ultimately supported by the minority working in the private sector.

---

[57] Willi Leibfritz, Deborah Roseveare, Douglas Fore and Echard Wurzel, *Aging Populations, Pension Systems and Government Budgets: How do they Affect Saving?* OECD Economics Department Working Papers n. 156, 1995.

1. Increase in Health-Care Costs

Health costs, although lower than retirement pensions, are still considerable. In 1992, the average health-care expenses of the European members of OECD was about 8% of GDP, a ratio lower than that of the U.S., but considerable and increasing. Furthermore, the larger European countries had the higher ratios -8.7%, 9.4% and 8.5% respectively. Among the large countries only the UK, at 7.1%, was below average.[58]

As a rule, the incidence of health-care costs on the over-65 population is much higher than for the rest of the population, as we can see in the following table.

TABLE 3

BREAKDOWN OF HEALTH CARE COSTS BY AGE GROUP IN OECD'S POPULATION IN 1993 (by %)

	Age 0-64		Age 65+		Age 75+	
	Population	Cost	Population	Cost	Population	Cost
United States	87.3	62.8	12.7	37.2	5.4	20.7
Japan	86.5	57.1	13.5	42.9	8.7	33.1
Germany	84.9	67.7	15.1	32.3	6.5	16.5
France	80.4	58.6	19.6	41.4	-	-
United Kingdom	84.4	58.0	15.6	42.0	6.8	27.1
Finland	86.2	61	13.8	38.5	5.7	22.1
Netherlands	86.9	60.1	13.1	39.9	-	-
Portugal	86.3	64.1	13.7	35.9	5.4	18.7
Sweden	82.5	62.2	17.5	37.8	8.1	21.4

(Source: OECD *Aging in OECD countries: a critical policy challenge, 1996,* OECD Social Policy Studies n° 20; p. 111).

---

[58] OECD. *New Directions in Health Care Policy,* 1995. OECD Health Policy Studies N° 7.

The obvious conclusion is that aging of Europe's population is going to make it difficult to contain health-care costs in the future.

2. PENSION SYSTEMS

According to Eurostat data for 1993, EU countries were spending on pensions in a range from 7.1% of GDP in Ireland to 19.1% in the Netherlands. Unfortunately, Ireland was something of an anomaly; pension costs in the largest countries, such as Germany, France and the United Kingdom were above 14% of GDP, and for Italy were over 17%.[59]

Pension systems, born after World War II in their modern form and expanded in the 1960s into their present configuration, no longer have the environments -economic growth and population growth- that once made them an attractive way to protect the population against poverty in old age. The number of workers financing the pay-as-you-go social security system has alarmingly diminished and will continue to decrease in the next decades. In addition, the increasingly higher public spending that they represent is responsible for serious economic distortions in European economies. Pensions (i) raise labor costs, thus removing incentives to hiring employees and fostering the informal economy; (ii) have a negative influence on domestic savings; (iii) yield future pensioners much less than what they would in a privately-run capitalized system, leaving aside the fact that their

---

[59]Philip E. Davis. Public Pensions, "Pension Reform and Fiscal Policy", European Monetary Institute, Staff Paper 5, March 1997.

security will be hostage to political and economic uncertainties. Although the assertion has been taboo in some European countries, such as Belgium or Spain, the present pension systems are unsustainable.

In the last few years, numerous studies have drawn attention to the problem, and some countries have decided to take measures. Most European countries, however, have decided, in view of other, more pressing problems, not to face up to the challenge of health-care and pension reform. In fact, there is widespread agreement that the effects of the inviability of pension systems will start to be felt in the next few years, and after 2010 will become very serious. (In Spain the unbalance is the greatest in Europe, except perhaps for Belgium and Sweden) [60]. By then, the consequences will be so dire that gradual measure will be futile. The necessary changes will be of such magnitude that it will take several years for our economies to recover, at the expense of lower growth and incalculable suffering.

In a recent study on pensions in the EU [61], the European Commission states that "transfers from workers to pensioners are increasing at a pace that is becoming unsustainable". This is because European pension systems are reaching maturity; that is, the number of pensioners is so high that workers can no longer continue to support them. At present, "there are fewer than four workers per pensioner, who finance his or her pension. By 2030 that number will be below

---

[60] See *El futuro de España,* pages 267-295.

[61] European Commission: *Modernizing and Improving Social Protection in the European Union,* 1997 (See also Simon Coss, "Survey: Social Europe Demographic Time Bomb Ticks Away" in European Voice, April 30-May 6, 1997).

two"[62]. In Spain the ratio are even more dramatic: it is already below two and by 2030 it will be lower than one.

According to OECD[63], the average increase in pension expenses as a percentage of GDP will range from 0.5 to 1.2 between 2000 and 2010. Thereafter, as the "baby boom" generation retires, the deterioration will become steeper. Thus, the estimated increase between 2010 and 2030 will average 2.0 to 2.3% of GDP, but will be higher for European countries.[64]

Another way to see what pension expenses represent is to calculate the net present value of each country's future pension commitments, or what is known as "implicit debt". Although the result depends on too many variables to offer mathematical reliability, it will provide us with an approximate idea of the magnitude of the problem. If we consider that the commitment entered into by states with their constituents represents a true debt, comparable to public debt, it is useful to measure the percentages that such commitments represent against the maximum 60% of Debt/GDP ratio which constitutes one of the five Maastricht Treaty criteria for qualification to EMU. OECD has made extremely interesting estimates on 1994 GDP which show the net present value of the differences between net pensions owed and contributions to be received by each country (see Table 4). The

---

[62]EU, European Commission. *Complementary Pension Systems in a Single Market, Green Book*. Brussels, October 10, 1997, COM (97) 283, 1997.

[63]Source: OECD. *Aging in OECD Countries: a Critical Policy Change*. 1996, OECD Social Policy Studies N° 20, pages 38-40.

[64]Danielle Franco and Teresa Munzi. *Public pension expenditure prospects in the EU: a survey of national projections*. In "Aging and Pension Expenditure Prospects in the Western World". EU/96, European Economy: reports and studies N° 3, pages 44-45.

result is negative for all countries, but varies considerably from one country to another. Thus, for Ireland or the UK, the liability for national accounts would be only 19% and 24% of GDP respectively. In contrast, it would exceed 100% of GDP, nearly twice the maximum allowed by Maastricht to be added to their national debt, for France, Spain, Portugal, Sweden and Belgium:

TABLE 4

DISCOUNTED NET COST OF PENSION COMMITMENTS AS PERCENTAGE OF GDP IN 1994 (OECD estimates)

	Gross Pensions	Contributions	Net Balance
United Kingdom	142	118	-24
Germany	348	286	-62
France	318	216	-102
Italy	401	341	-60
Belgium	300	147	-153
Denmark	234	n/a	n/a
Spain	323	214	-109
Finland	384	294	-65
Ireland	107	88	-19
Netherlands	214	161	-53
Portugal	277	168	-109
Sweden	369	219	-132

A study undertaken by the economic department of OECD[65] analyzes the effects that population aging, with

---

[65] Willi Leibritz, Deborah Roseveare, Douglas Fore and Eckard Wurzel. *Aging Populations, Pension Systems and Government Budgets. How Do They Affect Savings?* OECD Economics Department, Working Paper 156, 1995.

present pension systems, will have on primary accounts and debt in the four large European countries. The study concludes that three of the four -Germany, France and Italy- will have, by 2030, a debt much higher than their GDP. Italy's debt might approach twice, and Belgium's three times, their respective GDPs. As the World Bank underlines, "present payroll taxes will not be remotely sufficient to cover this debt"[66]. All these calculations, of course, do not even take into account higher health-care costs.

Possible solutions to this problem range from postponing the retirement age to capitalizing savings for pensions in amounts related to predetermined objectives. Thus, a public pension system would guarantee fairness and relieve poverty through a "minimum pension" while a private system based on individual freedom of choice would seek insuring that each person would save more than a set minimum, and would thus encourage savings, a prerequisite for growth in modern economies.

Pension reform is a difficult and not yet ripe political issue. Very few politicians in Europe declare themselves in favor of profound reform of the present pay-as-you-go systems, because to do so would be a sort of electoral suicide. An EU solution of the problem is unthinkable for two reasons. The first is that pension systems vary considerably from country to country and are, furthermore, of exclusive jurisdiction of member States. The second reason is that the Stability Pact agreed to as precondition for the EMU imposes budgetary constraints which limit the ability of states to assume a higher deficit or to borrow.

---

[66] World Bank. *Averting the Old Age Crisis. Policies to Protect the Old and to Promote Growth.* World Bank Policy Research Report, Oxford University Press, 1994.

It goes without saying that the longer a country goes without deciding on and implementing radical reform, respecting acquired rights but initiating a capitalization system, the worse will be the problem it eventually has to face.

In conclusion, population aging is going to force public pension systems to absorb an increasing proportion of public spending in the first half of the 21st century. Whether these systems are financed by increasing taxes or by borrowing, the economic impact will be -is already- very negative. If taxes are increased, job creation is discouraged, there is an incentive for early retirement and for the submerged economy, and national savings tend to decrease. Borrowing pushes interest rates upwards, flirts with inflation, dampens private investment and crowds out public investment in sectors as vital as education and infrastructures, both essential to economic growth.

(d) Problems of Governance

One disadvantage of the European Union compared with other industrialized countries, and particularly the United States, often goes unremarked in analyses of economic power and competitiveness: its governance. The fact that the U.S. and Japan are both nation-states, while Europe is still a conglomerate of countries that have been seeking, for more than forty years, an optimal formula for political and economic integration, constitutes a serious liability.

In such a situation, there is need for a figure, the most competent and least controversial possible, to be at the helm of the economic ship. In his contribution to the Gorbachev

Foundation Conference, James Tobin underlined the decisive influence of Alan Greenspan in the very positive economic performance of the United States in the last six years, and the relevance of this issue to the success or failure of the economies of industrialized countries during this decade [67]. The world economy has performed disappointingly; among advanced industrialized countries, the U.S. has been the star, boasting sustained growth without inflation or unemployment. Japan's economy has been stagnant in the 1990s and is currently (1998) mired in a recession; its situation is one of the keys to understanding the crisis of the Asian economies. Europe has become poorer relative to the U.S., with very low growth, controlled inflation but rising unemployment, and a massive devaluation of its currencies against the U.S. dollar.

James Tobin assigns considerable credit for the success of the U.S. economy to Alan Greenspan, president of the Federal Reserve. Tobin argues that many of the economic problems of other countries during this decade are due to the absence of a strong institution at the helm. Greenspan's success is evident and unquestioned. In contrast, the G-7 has abdicated its former function of supervising the world economy, the Bank of Japan has not been a factor, and the Bundesbank's leadership has been controversial in Europe.

Will the European Central Bank be successful at the helm of Europe's economy? Chapter V of this book looks at this issue and raises some doubts.

---

[67] James Tobin: *The Global Economy: Who is at the Helm?*, article presented to the Council for World Affairs in Springfield, Illinois, on October 23, 1997 and revised for the Gorbachev Foundation on December 15, 1997.

(e) Political Problems

To analyze and quantify Europe's political problems is a task that could fill volumes. I will limit myself to a brief list:

1. Despite the admirable results achieved since 1957, conflicts of interests among European countries still block the path towards political and economic integration.

2. The inability of Europe to adopt common external policies was evident in the former Yugoslavia, where the U.S. had to take the initiative.

3. The enlargement of the EU to the countries of Eastern Europe will have little immediate positive economic impact, adding only 5% to the EU's total GDP, although in the long term it will prove necessary and beneficial. In the short-term, it will result in a high net cost for the countries who are already members of the EU. Those whose per-capita GDP is higher than average will have to increase their contribution to the EU's budget; those who, like Spain, are below average will lose part of the subsidies they now receive from the EU.

4. Finally, it is useful to remember that the situation of our African neighbors on the other side of the Mediterranean is unstable, and that the costs of the detonation of what many consider a time bomb will fall on Europe. Again, the EMU is not relevant to the persistence of these problems.

Conclusions

The list of problems, most of which are more serious than those of other industrialized countries, has receded in the awareness of a Europe fascinated by the EMU. Some of these problems have been debated separately, but I have neither read nor heard, during the last five years, any systematic study of them or any serious proposals for their solution.

The book that Jesús Pérez and I are preparing for 1999 has as its objective to present a comprehensive assessment of the future of Europe, including proposed solutions to its problems. The aim of the present book is more modest: to defuse triumphalism and to reduce unrealistic expectations about the European Union. I think that the preceding chapter establishes two conclusions. First, in the medium and long term, Spain and Europe face a great many hurdles; while they are not insurmountable, they must be acknowledged and addressed. Second, despite the hopes that governments and media have placed in the Euro, it will prove to be largely irrelevant to surmounting those hurdles. None of the problems described in this chapter will be solved by the European Monetary Union.

V. PROSPECTS FOR THE EMU

(A) Economic Benefits of European Monetary Union

Although the principal objective of monetary union has always been political, there have also been attempts to justify it from an economic standpoint. Let us consider five such arguments.

1. ELIMINATION OF FOREIGN EXCHANGE TRANSACTION COSTS. The savings in foreign exchange commissions would almost balance out the corresponding losses suffered by banks and foreign exchange agencies. There would also be some bookkeeping savings for firms with operations in other European countries, since not having to deal with different currencies would simplify their accounting procedures. While not large, this advantage of monetary union is significant, implying a net savings in the range of 0.3-0.4% of the European GDP.

2. DIMINISHED PRICE UNCERTAINTY. Proponents of this advantage argue that it would translate into an increase in trade and investment between member nations due to the elimination of exchange risk. This would help to accelerate the

pace of industrial rationalization, since European firms will be able to see through the veil of different currencies in comparing prices. EMU's detractors, on the other hand, argue that this seemingly plausible advantage is fictitious; monetary union is not essential to eliminating uncertainty and increasing trade and investment. The historical relationship between Canada and the United States, two advanced, industrialized countries who share a common border, proves that having different currencies is no obstacle to an increasingly close economic relationship. It may be that the truth lies between these two positions: a common currency and the elimination of exchange risk would be somewhat advantageous for the business sector. Another advantage, potentially more significant, is the opportunity the Euro would provide for the unification and enlargement of European capital markets, which could thereby expand and become more efficient. But this result is not a certainty.

3. LONG-TERM MACROECONOMIC CREDIBILITY FOR COUNTRIES WITH WEAK CURRENCIES. This advantage would appear to be obvious for the countries of Southern Europe. Since 1996, the international financial markets have believed in the EMU project and expected monetary and fiscal discipline to result from its introduction. This market confidence has caused interest rates to fall in Spain, Italy, and Portugal, and has kept the peseta, the lira, and the escudo stable. In fact, our interest rates have fallen more rapidly than either the rate of inflation or the interest rates of countries with strong currencies, resulting in proportionately greater economic benefits for us.

The enemies of the EMU counter, not without reason, that this macroeconomic credibility may have been necessary in times of high inflation, as occurred immediately following the collapse of the system of fixed parities established at Bretton Woods; but that governments and independent central banks have over many years proven capable of maintaining this economic credibility for their nations without monetary union. As we will see, Jeffrey Sachs predicts that before long, the central banks of Spain and Italy will bitterly lament having inextricably linked themselves to the Bundesbank. [68]

4. THANKS TO THE EURO, EUROPE WILL INCREASE ITS WORLDWIDE PRESTIGE AND CLOUT, AND THE EURO WILL REPLACE THE DOLLAR AS THE RESERVE CURRENCY. Here again, there is disagreement between proponents and detractors of monetary union. Some players in the international financial markets think that the Euro will rival the dollar, which has enjoyed a privileged position as the world's reserve currency. Nevertheless, most believe that if this occurs, it will be a gradual process; it is unlikely that the new Euro will approach the level of confidence inspired by the dollar. Moreover, the elimination of historically strong national currencies such as the DM or the florin may reduce aggregate Euro reserves as compared with the total currently invested in EU currencies. Many bankers and financial executives with whom I have

---

[68] I present Jeffrey Sachs as spokesman for the majority. See "Europe Grows Apart" in *The Economist*, March 7-13 1998, pp. 75-76, which ends with the following statement: "The politicians who how enthusiasm about Europe's fledging Central Bank today are likely to be far less enamoured when that reality hits home."

spoken over the past twelve months think that EMU will result in large monetary flows toward the dollar or currencies of European countries who have not joined, such as the pound sterling or the Swiss franc.

One fact that leads many financial executives to conclude that the Euro will not rival the dollar as the world's reserve currency is the United States' fiscal and economic strength, with expected budget surpluses that stand in sharp contrast to European deficits of around 3%, and robust prospects for economic growth which exceed those of Europe. The analysis of Europe's problems that I presented in the previous chapter is not news to the financial sector. Jeffrey Sachs has predicted a future revaluation of the dollar against the yen and the Euro. My own conclusion, based on more than thirty years of professional experience, is that it is impossible to know whether or not the Euro will displace the dollar, or whether the Euro's value vis-à-vis the dollar will rise or fall.[69]

Commenting on many French writers's predictions of greater world influence for Europe thanks to the Euro, Jeffrey Sachs referred sarcastically to "being haunted all his

---

[69] In effect, even though experiences like those of George Soros would seem to refute my theory, the only lesson that I have learned is that it is impossible to predict the future rate of exchange between two important currencies. The one seemingly paradoxical exception is actually easy to understand: if all of the experts think that the dollar is going up, it will most certainly go down, while if all them agree that it is going down, it will almost surely go up. The reason for this is that the market adjusts expectations immediately, and the generalized belief that the dollar is going to go up indicates that it already has gone up. Therefore, the fulfillment of all of the parameters on which the prediction was based has already been taken into account; in the unlikely case that all of those parameters are fulfilled, the price of the dollar will not change, but if just one of them remains unfulfilled, it will move in the opposite of the predicted direction.

life by the thought of having to listen to the French give political opinions on economic topics." Sachs was referring to the delusions of grandeur expressed during a conference celebrating the centenary of the French franc and to French politicians' ill-fated insistence on maintaining a strong franc when it would have been highly beneficial for France, Germany, and Europe if its 1993 devaluation against the mark had taken place in 1988-89.

5. EUROPEAN UNION: GERMANY'S INFLUENCE IN EUROPE. This factor, as we saw in Chapter III, is more than an advantage -it was one motive for the creation of European Monetary Union. This argument is, of course, political rather than economic. I remember many conversations in the late eighties and early nineties with Paco Fernández Ordoñez, the Minister of Foreign Affairs who signed the Maastricht Treaty; through our talks, I followed the progress of the EMU's preparation. [70]

Immediately after the fall of the Berlin wall and the predicted re-unification of Germany at the beginning of 1990, Paco told me about the chill that had passed through the Council of Ministers of the European Union when suddenly Hans-Dietrich Genscher, the German Minister of Foreign Affairs, who had always spoken in English, began speaking

---

[70] I remember spending the whole morning together in his office in Santa Cruz on December 14, 1988, the day of the Spanish general strike. Paco told me about the visit of Vernon Walters, who had reported to the government of Felipe González on recent conversations that President Reagan and President-elect Bush had held with Gorbachev, raising the then incredible possibility of the end of the Cold War. We were trying to imagine the consequences of peace, which included the "peace dividend" - expected savings on the cost of armaments- and the growing power of Germany.

in German. The Ministers from Holland, Belgium and Luxembourg also switched to German and never reverted back to English. The psychological and political justifications for neutralizing Germany and integrating her into Europe certainly played a crucial role in the acceptance of monetary union, while the expectation of economic advantages rested on the perception of Germany as Europe's economic locomotive. As we saw in the previous chapter, this perception no longer holds sway.

(B) Economic Disadvantages of Monetary Union [71]

There are various very important economic arguments against EMU. The first is that it does not include provisions for secession or "divorce". The second is the naming of "optimal currency areas" which entail the loss of the market adjustment mechanism for each country's currency. The third, which fewer Europeans have considered, is the elimination of a national authority or "lender of last resort", which can intervene in a crisis.

The absence of procedures for a "divorce" -for example, if one or several countries feel that monetary union is damaging their economy and wish to revert to their own currency, or if the EMU desintegrates altogether- is a two-edged sword. On the one hand, it implies an eternal covenant based on faith and optimism. On the other hand, if serious tensions

---

[71] For important opinions against the implementation of monetary union voiced by non-American economists, see Alberto Recarte, *La UM: un proyecto peligroso, incompleto y precipitado,* and Pedro Schwartz, *Vade Retro: llamamiento a los ciudadanos europeos sobre la UM,* in *A favor y en contra de la moneda única,* Argentaria, Estudios de Política Exterior y Biblioteca Breve, Madrid, 1997.

or an acute crisis require a partial or total rupture, the resulting conflicts may be aggravated by the lack of a pre-established procedure for backing out of monetary union in an orderly manner.

As we will see, many American economists believe that the likelihood of divorce is very high. I believe that the pros and cons of the Euro's apparent irreversibility cancel each other out, and I am, however, convinced of the necessity of analyzing the following two problems.

1. Loss of fiscal and monetary sovereignty and the market mechanism: optimal currency areas

Monetary union means not only that each country must abandon the possibility of devaluing its currency and fixing interest rates, but also that it must give up its fiscal autonomy. This is not due solely to the Stability Pact, which obligates EMU members to control their budget deficits; the globalization and integration of Europe will make it imperative to gradually harmonize fiscal policy.

Implicit in the abandonment of this policy tool is the surrender of the market mechanism for determining the value of a nation's currency, which, like any tradeable good, has a price that is mediated by supply and demand. If that price is fixed from the start and the good disappears from the market, that country has abandoned the possibility of using the price of its currency to adapt. Detractors of EMU feel that to do away with market control of currency prices means eliminating the ultimate escape valve that allows weaker economies to recover their competitiveness.

It is certainly true that there are other ways of adapting to adverse changes: price and salary flexibility, labor force mobility, or a massive fiscal redistribution of funds to those zones hardest-hit by the changes. These are the measures that must be surrendered in an "optimal currency area," a term coined by the Canadian economist Robert Mundell in the 1960's [72]. We will briefly consider the requirements for a viable monetary union (and will conclude that while the United States, which adopted its monetary union in 1913, seems to meet them, the European Union does not).

(i) Price and Salary Flexibility: while the United States labor market is characterized by almost total flexibility, in Europe salaries, prices, and the labor market in general are exceedingly inflexible, as we have seen in the previous chapter's discussion of unemployment.

(ii) Labor Force Mobility: this is also much more evident in the United States than in Europe. When a steel mill closes in Pittsburgh, Pennsylvania, the vast majority of workers who have lost their jobs are willing to move to Texas, Massachusetts, California or wherever there are opportunities for employment. They can also support themselves on the second leg of "Reich's stool" [73] by investigating these opportunities through employment agencies or the Internet. In

---

[72] Robert Mundell, "A Theory of Optimum Currency Areas", *American Economic Review.* Volume 51, 1961.

[73] See Chapter IV.

Europe, because of language barriers, religious differences, or closer family ties, the opposite is more likely: with some exceptions [74], workers are much more reluctant to relocate, not only from one country to another, but also from one region to another, as is the case now in Germany. This aggravates long-term unemployment (the proportion of the unemployed who have been out of work for years), and also makes the introduction of monetary union more problematic.

(iii) Possibility of fiscal redistribution. When there is a crisis in one of the states of North America (as occurred in Texas with the drop in oil prices in the mid-eighties), the federal government can temporarily redistribute large amounts of funds to that state, thereby alleviating the effects of the recession. In Europe, one state cannot help another out of a recession and there is no fiscal redistribution mechanism, since the budget of the European Union represents scarcely 1.25% of European GDP.

(iv) Autonomous fiscal policy. In the United States the states have a certain fiscal margin, since they can establish their own taxes and can incur a deficit under adverse circumstances. In contrast, European

---

[74]The fact that Portugal's unemployment rate has remained low despite a reduction in the percentage of the population engaged in agricultural work can only be explained by the mobility of the labor force.

nations who are members of the EMU will not be permitted a deficit of more than 3%.

The conclusion of this analysis is that it will be much more difficult for the nations of Europe to live within a monetary union than it is for the American states. If asymmetric shocks occur -that is, if one of the European nations approaches recession or experiences serious difficulties due to the closing of important firms, a sector-specific crisis (such as in Spain's tourist industry) that affects one country more than another, or specific problems of whatever type- the nation in crisis will have no protection. The European Central Bank will not be able to modify its monetary policy to favor a minority to the detriment of the majority. The nation in crisis will be trapped in a blind alley. (Perhaps "on the edge of a cliff" would be more accurate).

There is a lot of truth to this argument, but there is no need to exaggerate its importance or to make it the basis for predicting that the EMU must be a catastrophe. I have two objections, not to this line of reasoning, but to the rejection of monetary union on this basis alone. First, such crises or asymmetric shocks are unlikely to occur. Second, "competitive devaluations" (those whose sole purpose is competitive gain) have been prohibited by the Rome Treaty for more than forty years.

An asymmetric shock in Europe would seem unlikely, since the various European countries produce, import, and export similar products and have very diversified economies. In fact, it could be said that the economies of the European countries are more similar to one another than are the economies of the individual states in the U.S. Nevertheless, the present argument cannot be easily discounted. It is important that the EMU's member countries have some market flexibility, and that they retain the capacity to adapt not only to a shock (which is by definition unforeseeable) but also to predictable differences in productivity between nations that may over time lead to disequilibrium and unemployment. This is especially true because one would expect a single currency to produce specialization, which would tend to discourage diversification. One example of a potential shock that would profoundly affect the Spanish economy without necessarily having any adverse effects on the other European countries would be a crisis in North Africa. The resultant instability in our country would affect tourism; one need only call to mind the vulnerability of this industry in such countries as Egypt, which has lost more than 80% of its principal source of foreign exchange and a significant portion of its GDP.

Another consideration that weakens the argument that monetary union will deny member nations the option of devaluing their currencies to increase competitiveness is that such devaluations have been prohibited since the establishment of the Common Market. For some reason, the American detractors of EMU ignore this fact. It is true that there have been devaluations in the forty-year history of the Common Market, but they have generally been in response to differences in inflation between countries, which in theory will not occur in the future. The argument that surrendering the ability to devalue is a significant sacrifice is refuted by Article 101 of the Rome Treaty, under which, if the Commission concludes that some country is distorting com-

been regulated for years by the 1988 Basle Capital Guidelines, which impose capitalization requirements that make severe banking crises impossible in Europe (as well as in the United States and the other signatory nations). [75]

But is it really unthinkable? The future is filled with events that will be considered unthinkable until they occur. And there is no lack of precedents. One need only go back as far as the seventies, when it was necessary to intervene in Bankhaus Herstatt[76]; more recently, there are the examples of Banesto in Spain and Credit Lyonnais in France. The banking systems of some European countries hardly impress one with their solidity. It would be unwise to believe that Europe is immune to an Asian-style crisis simply because the causal mechanisms would not be identical.

For Jeffrey Sachs[77], the crisis in the Asian economy that began during the summer of 1997 may be the precursor of a crisis in Europe. The Asian crisis resulted principally from the collapse of the banking system and from the fact that there was no institution capable of injecting it with the necessary liquidity. This situation was produced and aggravated, in my opinion, by the absence or inhibition of a bank of last resort -a Bank of Asia or a "Bank of the World." The International Monetary Fund does not seem to have played a constructive role, at least

---

[75] For a complete analysis of the Basle Guidelines, their implications, and their applicability to the banking sectors in emerging countries, see Marta Hidalgo, *Difficulties in the Application of Capital Adequacy Standards to Emerging Country Banking Sectors.* DFC, Spotlight, Fall 1997.

[76] Ibid, p. 2

[77] Conference (previously cited) on the European Monetary Union, Harvard University, January 27, 1998.

initially [78]. The consequences of the Asian crisis, which was all the more destructive for being completely unforeseen, will go deeper than was initially perceived, as we saw in the chapter on globalization.

Were a banking crisis to occur in one of our countries, it is doubtful that the European Central Bank would be able to intervene to pull that nation's banks, stockholders, and depositors out of the morass. How could it do so without being accused of partiality or favoritism by the other countries or by the banks' competitors? It seems to me that little or no attention is being paid to this problem, which has both political and economic aspects and is very likely to occur in the future of the EMU.

The restructuring of banks in crisis would result in severe deflationary pressures on the system [79]. Banking policy, which has been little discussed until now, will therefore become enormously important, and both stockholders and depositors will have to take into account the solvency of the institutions in which they plan to invest or deposit their money before making a selection.

Conclusion

As the discussion in Chapter IV also demonstrated, the EMU will resolve none of our fundamental problems; on the

---

[78] See Martin Feldstein's article "Refocusing the IMF", about the International Monetary Fund's errors in the Asian crisis, in *Foreign Affairs,* March-April 1998, which in my opinion makes much more sense than his article on the Monetary Union published in the fall 1997 edition of Foreign Affairs.

[79] Jeffrey Sachs, conference cited, January 27, 1988.

contrary, it tends to aggravate them. Considered in isolation and in exclusively economic terms, monetary union offers opportunities and dangers that are difficult to quantify. While its advantages are not likely to be as substantial as its defenders claim, its costs are not likely to be as enormous as its detractors predict. The advantages are limited to savings in transaction costs and to greater integration, assuming that the Euro motivates firms to cross borders. The potential disadvantages are much more important, but the likelihood of their occurring is uncertain. The European Monetary Union is a zero-sum game at best, and it must be justified in political rather than economic, terms.

(C) Political Arguments in Favor of Monetary Union

Some of the political explanations for the genesis of the EMU were examined in Chapter III, which summarized the project's historical evolution. It will be useful to review them here and to consider whether they are still applicable and are likely to continue driving monetary union toward introduction and success.

(i)   GEOPOLITICAL ARGUMENTS. The Franco-German pact and the desire to avoid a history of conflict was a powerful reason behind the creation of the European Union. The EMU is an attempt to deepen this union. The unified currency and its effects in other sectors would give the French a sense of control over Germany and assure them that the two nations have sufficient common interests to prevent Germany

111

from swinging toward the East, which might lead to economic, political, and even military conflict. Germany's continuing post-World War II sense of responsibility would lead to a new demonstration of commitment to a unified Europe.

Will this project of alliance and mutual control continue? Will it outlive such individuals as Chancellor Helmut Kohl, who have pledged their political capital to its accomplishment? Jeffrey Frieden, a Harvard political scientist, has pointed out that integration the French and German armies might be a more effective way to achieve the same goals [80]. Nor does the geopolitical factor explain why European countries, except for the United Kingdom and Scandinavia, are so interested in joining the Monetary Union, or whether their continued support is assured.

(ii) ECONOMIC AND POLITICAL CREDIBILITY OF COUNTRIES WITH WEAK CURRENCIES. France, Spain, and Portugal, countries with a history of price instability, have an interest in demonstrating their ability to control inflation. Their entry into the EMU represents an important step.

This motivation was important in the 1980's and until 1995. Now, however, this credibility has been established; all these countries have managed to lower inflation to around 2% per year. It does not appear that this goal will play such

---

[80]Conference at Harvard previously cited, January 27, 1998.

an important role in the future or that it will contribute to keeping the EMU together.

(iii) CORE AND PERIPHERY. This is the most important reason. The European nations have shown a keen interest in joining the EMU not -or not only- because it attracts or convinces them, but because membership is a prerequisite to being considered a first-class citizen within the European Union. Members of the EMU club will have a voice in decisions that will crucially influence even more important matters, such as the requirements for deepening and widening the European Union.

This is the bottom line: a nation that is excluded from the EMU could lose influence in the other EU institutions. Although it would continue to be a member with all of the corresponding rights, it is the core of the European Union, and not the periphery, that will have most to say about decisions of significance. Even the United Kingdom has expressed apprehension about not participating in the informal conversations that the ministers of finance of the EMU member nations will hold. Some nations feared losing foreign investors if they stayed out of the Monetary Union. Another consideration was the expected additional cost an difficulty of banking and trade transactions with EMU members.

This desire not to be left out will continue to play a motivating role as long as the European Monetary Union is perceived to be a success. But if it is not successful, what is to prevent the departure of one nation from provoking a stampede and an "every man for himself" situation?

(iv) POLITICAL PRESSURES WITHIN EACH COUNTRY. The European electorate has received little information about EMU. Among those who have interested themselves in the subject, the international trade and investment sectors have been in favor of Maastricht, while civil servants, public-sector employees, and unions have come out against it.

In general, the supporters of monetary union have been more influential than its detractors. The business sector of nearly every country has been in favor of monetary union, and has lobbied for convergence policies[81]. Will businessmen and bankers continue to support monetary union? Probably, unless there is a crisis severe enough to make it more profitable to undo what has been done. It is likely, however, that there are within each nation sectors that have not yet formed organized lobbies, who will blame their difficulties -whether they are in fact caused by monetary union or are simply the unavoidable result of Europe's current problems- on the Euro. It is difficult to predict which tendency will prevail.

(D) Success and Failure: Possible Scenarios

INTEGRATION AND DECENTRALIZATION

The eminent political scientist Stanley Hoffman has put forth an institutional theory that is relevance here. In both the

---

[81] I have first-hand knowledge of the case of the CEOE in Spain and its president José María Cuevas, and also of the French employers' association, where enthusiasm for monetary union has been more tempered.

European Union and the EMU there are two competing dynamics: integration and decentralization. On one hand, the economy demands an ever-increasing degree of coordination and centralization to assure stability and security; accordingly, the European states have decided to surrender their monetary sovereignty and to the European Central Bank. On the other hand, politics demands a significant degree of deference to the citizenry. Europe's institutions are becoming increasingly democratic; citizens directly elect members of the Parliament, and the Council is made up of indirectly-elected representatives. These two forces have coexisted for at least the past fifty years without any great friction. Nevertheless, in the accelerated world of today, the EMU could turn out to be a leap forward that national politicians will come to regret.

It appears likely to me that this tension between political decentralization and economic integration will eventually undermine the EMU. The processes that will be set in motion will be of such a magnitude as to make frictions unavoidable. It is not hard to imagine one country -France, for example- resentful of the economic effects of monetary union (unemployment, for example), deciding to act on its prerogative as a nation and let the others know who is going to have the last word. This eventuality became even more credible on May 2-3 with the French stubborn insistence to limit the tenure of the ECB's first governor. In any case, as each nation's citizens become more zealous every day about defending their rights, the likelihood of political union recedes. That would require a new constitution for Europe and for each member of the EU, a redistribution of powers and

Our future depends on two fundamental parameters: one is the continued dominance of an international political and economic order based on Darwinian, competitive capitalism; the other is whether or not we Europeans are capable of effecting the reforms necessary to resolve the problems, analyzed in Chapter IV, that darken Europe's horizon.

If *The Future of Europe,* which will appear in 1999, were published today (i.e., in the summer of 1998), it would probably present four scenarios for Europe in the first fifteen years of the twenty-first century:

. an optimistic scenario, which assumes that Europeans are capable of turning outward and of putting "the three legs" on Reich's stool, by reducing unemployment, reforming the pension system, improving our university education, recovering part of the ground we have lost in the realm of technology, and revitalizing and increasing the competitiveness of our private sector. Given these hypothetical achievements, I believe that EMU could be a success, despite its dangers;

. a moderately optimistic scenario, in which the necessary reforms are effected slowly as the governments and electorates of the European nations, caught between a rock and a hard place, become convinced of the necessity of confronting the status quo. In this case, I believe that there would be debate over the EMU, that the process of European integration would cause disillusionment and would be blamed for any persistent problems, but that the Euro would survive;

117

a pessimistic scenario in which we Europeans are not able to implement critical reforms: the monetary policy of the European Central Bank, together with a gradual decrease in European firms' ability to compete, leads to rising unemployment; economic growth stagnates, governments lose tax revenue and are faced with pressures to increase spending which they cannot contain; or there is an important crisis in one of the countries (probably France)[82] –including social protests and strikes similar to or even more severe than those of the fall of 1995– that infects other nations with disgust for the European Commission; or an asymmetric shock in which one country is hit with a severe crisis; or one of the nations decides to secede from the Monetary Union and to revert back to its own currency; or there is a conflict between Germany and France that proves difficult to resolve. As a result, the EMU is dissolved, the general conviction is that it was not a worthwhile undertaking, and the waters in the end return to their source;

the catastrophic scenario postulated by Martin Feldstein, in which the crises described in the pessimistic scenario reach paroxysmal proportions and the failure of the Monetary Union ends up unleashing military conflicts, first within Europe and later spreading to the United States.

---

[82] This pessimistic scenario for France is the subject of François de Closets, *Le Compte a Rebours* (Fayard, 1998) which contemplates a 15% unemployment rate in France, a withdrawal of France from EMU in 2001, and an electoral victory of the Front National in 2002.

I do not think my readers will find any of these four scenarios wildly implausible. The critical question is: What is the probability that any one of them will come to pass?

In the January 1998 conference at Harvard, the author put this question to Jeffrey Sachs. The scenarios were three, labelled "optimistic", "pessimistic", and "neutral". Much to the astonishment of the attendees, Sachs [83] not only answered the question, but did so almost without hesitation: "As I see it, the likelihood that monetary union will have a truly positive effect on Europe and the world is 10%; that its effect will be neutral, and it will live on without pain or glory is 50%, and that it will be bad or very bad for Europe is 40%." This position coincided with that of the other members of the academic community: the most likely outcome -neutral- was given a 50% probability, but negative outcomes were considered far more likely than positive ones.

Perhaps a person who authors such scenarios should not favor one of them over another, but should let the reader reach a decision based on the analysis presented. I am going to break this rule by assigning probabilities to my four scenarios. Although I am less negative than the Americans in judging the EMU in isolation, I am pessimistic about the ability of us Europeans to resolve our structural problems immediately. I therefore give a 5% probability to the optimistic scenario, 60% to the moderately optimistic, and 35% to the pessimistic. A catastrophe is always possible, but I

---

[83] It is a well-known fact that economists rarely stick their necks out by making predictions. A certain United States President said that he wanted only one-handed economists (so that they couldn't constantly say "on the one hand...on the other hand...").

cannot assign a percentage probability to the scenario of military conflict described by Feldstein.

The refutation of the plausibility of catastrophic outcomes is elegantly presented by Timothy Garton Ash, who gives three reasons. First, "the powerful neo-Kantian argument that bourgeois democracies are unlikely to go to war against each other. Second, unlike pre-1945 Europe, we have a generally benign extra-European hegemon in the United States. Third, to warn of violence is to ignore the huge and real achievement of European integration to date: the unique, unprecedented framework and deeply ingrained habits of permanent institutionalized cooperation which ensure that conflicts of interest between member states are never resolved by force. All these endless hours and days of negotiations in Brussels between ministers of fifteen European countries who end up knowing each other almost better than they know their own families: that is the essence of Europe. It is an economic community, of course, but it is also a security community –a group of states that find it unthinkable to resolve their own differences by war"[84]. I would add that the young generations of Europeans who have studied and worked in countries other than their own and continue to do so, thereby establishing relations of friendship throughout Europe in unprecedented and increasing ways, reduce the war scenario to the absurd.

---

[84] Timothy Garton Ash. "Europe's Endangered Liberal Order", *Foreign Affairs,* March-April 1998, p. 61.

VI. CONCLUSIONS

Once the overly optimistic and the catastrophic scenarios are dismissed we are left with two basic questions. What are the main factors that could allow the EMU to overcome difficulties and survive? And how can we, Europeans, contribute to enable the desirable and moderately optimistic scenario to win over the pessimistic one? I reject determinism and believe that, fortunately, both questions have clear answers.

The first one is that the success or failure of the EMU depends, to a great extent, on the expectations it creates. I agree with Ralf Dahrendorf that the EMU is irrelevant to the solution of European problems; thus, the more is expected from it, the more disappointing it will prove to be. It is understandable that governments of countries such as Spain, Portugal or Italy, that only two years ago seemed certain to be excluded from the EMU by the Maastricht criteria, now try to get credit for their success in being admitted; moreover, their life outside the EMU would be even harder than inside it. However, the excessive expectations that these governments and the media have raised in their citizens will eventually turn against the EMU. The risk that electorates will go to the extremes of the political spectrum, and that some irresponsible politicians will blame the EMU for all of Europe's problems, is very high.

The second answer is that we, Europeans, must realize that we are evolving within a global context. We must not only moderate our expectations but also be aware that it is up to us, and not to the Euro, to solve the problems that threaten the future of Europe.

BIBLIOGRAPHY

BARBER, LIONEL. *EU summit urged to agree targets for training jobless.* Financial Times, September 4, 1997.

BRITTAN, SIR LEON. *EMU: Prospects and Problems.* Speech to Conference on EMU at Royal Institute of International Affairs, London, March 14, 1996.

BUITER, W.H., CORSETTI, G.M., AND ROUBINI, M. *Excessive Deficits: Sense and Nonsense in the Treaty of Maastricht.* Economic Policy, 1993.

CAMERON, DAVID. *European Union and Unemployment.* Paper for lecture at the Center for European Studies, Harvard University, February 13, 1998.

CARLSON, RICHARD, AND GOLDMAN, BRUCE. *Fast Forward.* Harper Business, 1994.

CLOSETS, FRANÇOIS DE. *Le Compte a Rebours.* Fayard, 1998.

COSS, SIMON. *Survey: Social Europe Demographic Time Bomb Ticks Away.* European Voice, April 30, 1997.

CROTTY, JIM, AND EPSTEIN, GERALD. In *Defense of Capital Controls.* New York: Monthly Review Press, 1996, pp. 118-149.

DAHRENDORF, RALF. *From Europe to Europe: A Story of Hope, Trial and Error.* The Fifteenth Annual Paul-Henri Spaak Lecture, CFIA, Harvard University, October 2, 1996.

DAVIS, PHILIP E. *Public Pensions, Pension Reform and Fiscal Policy, European Monetary Institute.* Staff Paper 5, March 1997.

THE ECONOMIST. *On TIMMS.* April 29, 1997.

THE ECONOMIST. *Action Man.* September 13, 1997.

THE ECONOMIST. *Economic Indicators and Business Costs.* January 24, 1998.

THE ECONOMIST. *Europe Grows Apart.* March 7, 1998.

EUROPEAN COMMISSION. *Modernizing and Improving Social Protection in the European Union.* 1997.

EUROPEAN COMMISSION. *Complementary Pension Systems in a Single Market, Green Book.* COM (97) 283, October 10, 1997.

FELDSTEIN, MARTIN. *EMU and International Conflict.* Foreign Affairs, November-December 1997.

FELDSTEIN, MARTIN. *Refocusing the IMF.* Foreign Affairs, March-April 1998.

FRANCO, DANIELLE AND MUNZI, TERESA. *Public pension expenditure prospects in the EU: a survey of national pro-- jections.* Aging and Pension Expenditure Prospects in the Western World. European Commission, EU 96, Reports and Studies nº 3, 1996.

GARTON ASH, TIMOTHY. *Europe's Endangered Liberal Order.* Foreign Affairs, March-April 1998.

HAVEL, VACLAV. *How Europe can Fail.* Lecture at the Council of Europe, Vienna, November 9, 1993, quoted in New York Review of Books, November 18, 1993.

HIDALGO, DIEGO. *El futuro de España.* Taurus, Madrid, 1996.

HIDALGO, DIEGO. *The European Monetary Union: the conflict of creating "first" and "second class citizens" in the EU.* DFC Spotlight, Spring 1997.

HIDALGO, MARTA. *Difficulties in the Application of Capital Adequacy Standards to Emerging Country Banking Sectors.* DFC Spotlight, Fall 1997.

IMF. *World Economic Outlook,* 1998

KAPSTEIN, ETHAN B. *Workers and the World Economy.* Foreign Affairs, May-June 1996.

KLAU, THOMAS. *Germany edges toward deregulation.* European Voice, April 30-May 6, 1997.

KAUFMANN, HUGO. *European Economic Monetary Union. Prospects and pitfalls. Is EMU premature?* Paper presented at the Third World-ECSA Conference in Brussels, September 19-20, 1996.

LEIBFRITZ, WILLI, ROSEVEARE, DEBORAH, FORE, DOUGLAS AND WURZEL, ECHARD. *Aging Populations, Pension Systems and Government Budgets: How do they Affect Savings?* OECD, Working Paper 156, 1995.

LEVINE, ROBERT A. *The Euro Will Arrive, but Then Be Aware of the Deluge.* IHT, April 25-26. 1998.

LEVINE, ROBERT A. *Not with a Bang But a Whimper: Western Europe Approaches the Third Millenium.*

MUNDELL, ROBERT. *A Theory of Optimum Currency Areas.* American Economic Review. Volume 51, 1961.

NEWHOUSE, JOHN. *Europe Adrift.* Pantheon Books, 1997.

OECD. *New Directions in Health Care Policy.* Health Policy Studies, n° 7, 1995.

OECD. *Aging in OECD Countries: A Critical Policy Change.* OECD Social Policy Studies n° 20, 1996.

OECD. *Employment Outlook.* July 1997.

RAZEN, ASSAF AND YEN, CHI-WA. *Labor Mobility and Fiscal Coordination.* Research Paper n° 5433, National Bureau of Economic Research, January 1996.

SACHS, JEFFREY. Lecture at Conference on EMU organized by the Weatherhead Center for International Affairs and the Center for European Studies, Harvard University, January 27, 1998, Proceedings published by WCFIA/CES, Harvard University, 1998.

SAINT-PAUL, GILLES. *Employment Protection, International Specialization and Innovation.* IMF Working Paper, WP/96/16, International Monetary Fund, February 1996.

SCHMIEDING, HOLGER. *Good Bye to Core EMU in 1999?* Merrill Lynch, Euro Strategy, February 28, 1997.

TOBIN, JAMES. *The Global Economy: Who is at the Helm?* Council for World Affairs, Springfield, Illinois, and Gorbachev Foundation, 1997

TUCKER, EMMA. *Workers Pay for Europe's Rigidities.* Financial Times, February 13, 1998.

WORLD BANK. *Averting the Old Age Crisis. Policies to Protect the Old and to Promote Growth.* Oxford University Press, 1994.